A Woman's Song

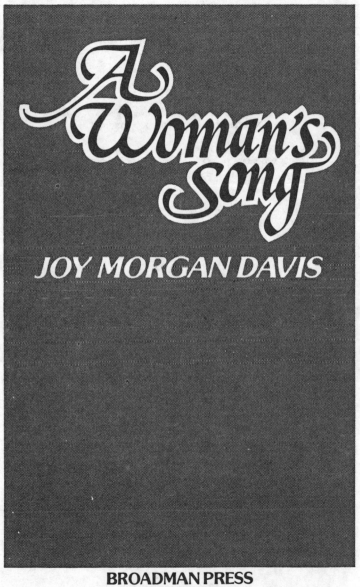

A Woman's Song

JOY MORGAN DAVIS

BROADMAN PRESS
Nashville, Tennessee

© Copyright 1983 • **Broadman Press**
All rights reserved
4252-43
ISBN: 0-8054-5243-5
Dewey Decimal Classification: B
Subject Headings: DAVIS, JOY MORGAN / / WOMEN
Library of Congress Catalog Card Number: 83-70376
Printed in the United States of America

Unless otherwise noted, Scripture quotations are from the
King James Version of the Bible.

Scripture quotations marked (Amp) are from **The Amplified Bible,**
Old Testament. Copyright © 1962, 1964 by Zondervan Publishing House.
Used by permission.

CREDIT: Photo of Joy Morgan Davis on back panel of book by Gary Bright

To
"Munler," my mother
Drew Ann, my daughter
Shannon, my daughter-in-love
and little Amber Leigh, my GRANDdaughter!

Love Letter to a Friend

MY DEAR:

I know how a woman's heart beats! I know how it opens to let in the love and how it hurts and breaks. I know how a woman's heart mends because it must!

I know the intimate tempo of the moments. I know laughter so light it gleams like gold! And I know tears that glisten in the dark like diamonds laid softly on the lashes.

I would know all of these riches if for no other reason than that I am a woman. But I have gathered, through the years, the riches of countless other women across our magnificent country! They have confided in me. They have been candid, open, and opinionated. They have befriended me. In heart-to-heart conversation, they have shared with me. They have shown me that women everywhere want more than ever to be caring, as well as confident! They want to learn how to love and how to face the future without fear; above all, they want to be the best WOMEN they can be! How marvelous!

My entrée into the "world of women" has been through the fun and fascinating way I spend my days! I am what the society sections of newspapers describe (rather loosely) as a "popular public speaker." That's as close as you can come, I suppose, to describing what I do; but it doesn't quite cover it. I read books and review them. I dress in costume and dramatize the characters and the plots, do scenes from plays, and talk about actresses and authors. I have a grand time. I'm a storyteller (I read and review them, I don't write them), and I am specifically a *woman's* storyteller. Whether I'm doing a new Christian novel for a group of church women or a secular best-seller for a woman's club, you can count on romance from me! I adore history and "period pieces." I do adventure tales too! But there is *always* romance in the truest, dearest, deepest sense of the word. Women respond in the most special way to romance! We are friends, confidantes at once, my audience and me, for I'm saying what they've felt for years. They laugh and cry with me on stage. Later, in empty auditoriums or deserted dressing rooms or on planes or over luncheon plates, they talk to me. They tell me who they are and what they want. And they tell me secrets because I am there only for a day, often only for a few hours, and therefore their secrets are safe with me!

I know, believe me, how a woman's heart beats. And this book is for you but mostly for me because I want to be the best woman I can be!

Contents

Section I
The Joyful Song Begins

My entrée into the world of women comes from the fun, fascinating way I spend my days. Mine is a career that has led me across the country into the lives of hundreds of women! They have confided in me, cried with me, laughed with me, become my friends. The view from my vantage point into feminine hearts, minds, and emotions has been poignant, beautiful, and blessed.

My father wrote seldom (preferring, usually, to *say* the words), so I saved his letters like silver dollars. They were rare! His ministry was in music, and on his stationery was a music staff, with notes climbing up and down and around the staffs. Beneath the notes there was a Scripture, "Make a joyful noise unto the Lord, . . . serve the Lord with gladness: come before his presence with singing" (Ps. 100:1-2). That line from my father's stationery has become the statement of my life! I want more than anything else on earth to make a joyful noise unto the Lord! (Those who know me say this is because it would be impossible for me to make a joyful *silence* unto the Lord!)

That is true. I love to talk. I was born to talk. It's my destiny! I'm terrific at it! I can talk anytime, anywhere! I can talk first thing in the morning or last thing at night! I am what you could call an EXPRESSive person! I can talk eating, sleeping, whatever! You've heard of "kiss and tell"? Well *I* can kiss and *talk*, at the same time! (Well, almost.) I can talk myself into trouble and out again. Whatever is happening to me at the moment, my reaction to it is to talk. Glad, sad, mad—I talk. Sometimes I am fun to listen to, and sometimes I am not, especially if you live with me all the time. My husband used to mentally tune me out (or at least lower the

11

tone a little). I guess he thought I would wind down with age. He was wrong. As I have aged, I have had backaches, stomachaches, and headaches, but my mouth has never ached! We have now been married almost thirty years. *Now*, sometimes, he tells me to be quiet. Sometimes I do it.

Sometimes I talk so much I forget to listen to myself, and that can be dangerous. One summer Saturday my husband and I took to the lake. The day was hot, dry, dusty, and we made the great escape. (In Texas it is hot and dry even on the water, but at least it isn't dusty!) Jewell's new ski boat was beautiful, and we skimmed across the water feeling a breeze for the first time in a week. At last we anchored in a calm cove, thinking to cool off with a swim. (That's float for me, since I can't swim. But I can float pretty fast!) We eagerly snapped on our ski jackets and stood on the back of the boat, poised for the plunge. I was, naturally, talking, telling Jewell something of the greatest importance, I'm sure, but I wasn't listening to myself! When I jumped into the water, my mouth was in the middle of a sentence! After sinking four feet under, I bobbed to the surface, eyes wild, arms waving. I could not breath at all! I was like a pitcher somebody had just poured full! Jewell hurriedly hauled me in and hung me over the side of the boat by my middle, forcing the lake out of my lungs. Finally he turned me around and sat me down. His expression could have been called exasperated. "JOY!" he said severely, as if to a slow-witted child. "For just the thirty seconds that it takes you to jump into the water, you have *got* to stop *talking*!"

Not only do I talk but I also talk loudly. When I was a child, people noticed me, not because I was pretty or talented or intelligent but because I was noisy. My teachers commented on it. The neighbors complained. One boy signed my college annual, "Yes, I *heard* you." My parents got earmuffs for emergencies, like when they had to think.

Now that I am grown, people still notice me and for the same reason. I am noisy. Mainly it's my voice. I realized long ago that the volume of my voice must have been turned up before I was born. This is a great boon to a public speaker, which is what I turned out to be, but when you are growing up it's a bother. (Just try to whisper some secret to your date in the middle of the movie or ask your mother what's for dinner during church. And librarians have *never* liked me.)

I am not soft spoken. I laugh and sing and cry loudly. I *live* loudly. I don't even suffer in silence. I weep and wail. When I'm sick, I call all my friends and tell them I'm dying. As a result, there is a steady stream of people coming through the door with chicken soup and jello. When I am well, we celebrate loudly!

I have learned to live with it. There have been times when I have thought that to change would be an attainable challenge. No more. Life with me is just naturally noisy. The best I can do is to make it a joyful noise, and I try, I truly do try!

1
They Pay You for That?

Dallas, Texas, is the only town I know where people are paid for talking. Since that is the only thing I do really well, I am delighted to be in "Big D"!

Other cities have women's clubs and garden clubs and bridge clubs, Lionesses of the Lions, and the Junior League. Dallas has all of these, plus book clubs. Some several hundred book clubs are scattered throughout the Dallas-Fort Worth metroplex. These book clubs sponsor a speaker each month to read and review a book! They are sizable social and cultural assets to the cities! Book clubs began in the 1930s, when women of "letters" would entertain at "silver teas" to raise contributions to "the arts." The oral book review, from a gifted orator, is far from stuffy and staid. It is as moving as a Sarah Bernhardt performance! So fascinating was this form of entertainment that the book club was born in Dallas, and from the country clubs to the suburbs, groups of women gathered to listen and to learn and to be "well read"!

This, then, is the perfect place for me to be! I love to dress up and play lady! First it was for the book clubs. From the book clubs, I began to get calls for me and my costumes to go to the women's clubs, garden clubs, forums, and symphony

15

leagues throughout the country. And of course, church women do adore Christian drama, and I was called often for church women's societies! Meanwhile, no matter where or what the book, there was always the romance, and women were becoming more and more responsive to me. The view from my vantage point into feminine hearts, minds, and emotions has been poignant, tender, touching; and I have been blessed!

It has been fun, these fifteen years, for me and for my family. My husband is a remarkable man who has been proud and supportive. His love has "liberated" me. Maybe he "lets me go" because he knows so well that being his wife is always *first* with me! He cares for me, materially, as well as every other way. And I care for him. If I must be away one night, his meal is cooked, ready to heat and eat. His clothes are clean. His household is in order. And there is a love letter under his pillow!

Although I perform almost every day during "the season," September to May, most of my work is in the metroplex, which means I am away from home for only a few hours. Even when engaged in other states, I can fly to and from within one day and one night. Before the children were grown and gone, there was breakfast with everybody. There was the dash to get Dad to the office and Son and Daughter to the school, with books and jackets and tennis rackets before the first bell. At the end of the day, there was another dash—this time to music, tennis matches, and church and choir.

But in between, I turned myself into Someone Else! I added lots of lashes and Scarlett O'Hara hair, and for a few hours I was smack in the middle of some marvelous adventure! And in love! Always in love!

Now, without the children, it's not such a rush to turn into Scarlett or Katie Hepburn or Agatha Christie or the

Samaritan woman at the well, or whomever! (And it's a good thing because it takes me longer these days!) But it's still a marvelous adventure!

I have the most intriguing introduction to people! I talk, and they listen! I love it!

2
The Perils of a Public Speaker
Are Not Without Pitfalls

I have an admission to make. I love dogs and cats and canaries only in certain places, like somebody else's lap, on a Hallmark card, in the movies.

When I was growing up, we had two dogs at different times and at least one cat. They were a *lot* of trouble. Lovable but a *lot* of trouble. They weren't pedigreed or grand, just good old country dogs and cats. One of our dogs was named Toby. Toby, as I remember, chased chickens. He came to a very bad end. And one of our cats was named Fluffy. Fluffy did have some kind of papers, I believe. She was Persian. And I must admit she did look rather regal, stalking about the house with her tail up in the air like the queen of Siberia in her best sable. We got Fluffy when she was just a kitten. I mean she was just a *little* kitten, a ball of fur. One day Daddy picked her up and put her on the desk where he was working. She wet all over his papers. I was only seven, but I wondered *then* why we wanted her. Daddy, however, was amused and mopped up after her with a tissue. Fluffy, too, came to a bad end. One day she came down out of her ivory tower and played in the street.

My children had a dog. He was a pedigreed Chesapeake

Bay retriever, but we didn't have the papers. My husband and son found him as a puppy on a golf course in front of some elegant houses. He had all the markings of wealth and background and breeding (the vet said so); but when they found him, he was wet and cold and covered with ticks. They brought him home and put him in a warm box in the kitchen with a light and a clock for company to keep him from crying. We put ads in all the papers for days and days. Nobody claimed him, so he was our dog. The children called him Tic. Tic did not stay little for long. He grew huge. And *he* was a lot of trouble. Children are supposed to learn love and responsibility from having a dog. Actually, our children already knew about love and responsibility.

About the only thing they learned from Tic was that cod-liver oil makes strong bones. They learned it as all of us struggled to hold Tic down while I tried to pour a capful of cod-liver oil into him twice a day.

I thought I was through with dogs, cats, and canaries. Then I started book reviewing. I have discovered that a book club meeting is no place for pets. Contrary to what their owners believe, they are not "people," and they do not care about my book, not the hero or the heroine or the mystery or the romance! Most especially do they not care about whether the club will get its money's worth out of me.

You see, some book clubs meet in large halls with hundreds of people; others have small memberships and meet in neighborhoods, in each other's homes. Many of these homes come equipped with pets. Only on rare occasions have pets been NO problem. A few times I have had them lie down at my feet and sleep through the whole thing. I have had them wander off into the den and watch television. Once in a while, they will even leave the house, bored with the whole business. But these instances are few and far between! Mostly they are just excited to see everyone! Their people are having a party, and they want to be there! What fun! BARK, bark! PURR, purr!

Sometimes pets are put in the bathroom. This results in a lot of loud crying, howling, or mewing until they are finally let out, to lie at my feet. Sometimes they are put outside, (when they want to be inside). This results in a frantic scratching at the French doors or a thunderous thumping of the tail on the patio picture window until finally they are let in, to lie at my feet.

Some dogs are just unforgettable. (Unforgivable too, but we will move right along.) One scottie I remember had been trained to bark energetically and run around the room each time the Cowboys scored a touchdown. The dog did not understand the game plan on TV, of course. He simply responded to the applause of the people in the room. The day I appeared in that home, I was doing a patriotic program. There was *lots* of applause! Each and every time that dog dashed in from the den, barked energetically, and ran around the room! And *each* time his mistress remarked, adoringly, "He thinks the Cowboys have scored!" You would have thought that woman would have been mortified. But why be embarrassed? He was her dog, and she adored him!

Poodles are especially popular at Christmas, it seems. You would be surprised to know how many poodles wear jingle bells during the Christmas season. Granted, they are *little* bells on *little* dogs, but little bells can make a big noise in a room that is quiet. The poodle comes prancing in, always at the most climactic moment, like Tinker Bell on tiny painted toes! Immediately all eyes move from me to Tinker Bell, and "Mumsy" smiles sweetly as "Baby" leaps into her lap! Merry Christmas!

Cats are usually quieter than dogs, but they can be more

cunning. They wander around under the tables and chairs and tickle people unawares. Giggle, giggle. But one cat reminded me of a miniature cat of the jungle. She was all glorious gold and sleek, with emerald green eyes. She had been curled in front of the fire when I began to speak, and she looked settled in for a long winter's nap. But somewhere toward the end of my speech, she woke up and wanted her water. She looked around bewildered. There were fifty women sitting between her and the hall which led to her water. Hesitating only briefly, she backed up, arched herself high, and screeching like one of her jungle cousins, she took a flying leap *over* the couch. She flew between the heads of two terrified ladies and landed on the polished hardwood floor behind the couch, skidding through the door and down the hall! I concluded the book, but by then nobody cared. We did not see Tabby again that day. She undoubtedly decided to stay put and protect her water bowl from intruders. But if anybody knows of a feline jumping contest anywhere, I know a cat that could take the cup!

Cats and dogs are not the only form of disturbance by far. A lot of houses have pet parakeets. And there was the case of the canary who sang, even after his mistress covered his cage with a pillow case. "He *always* sleeps with the pillow case," she assured me. But that day he didn't. Gurgling fish tanks are the absolute limit. You can *remove* a pet, but if you unplug a fish tank for long, the fish will float to the top. Gurgle, gurgle.

My favorite fish story happened in a mansion. Dallas has lots of mansions, as anyone who watches television must know by now, and I have seen many of them. It is one of the bonuses of my business. I never have to buy a ticket to the Home and Garden Tour. I've already seen those places, and not only the downstairs but also the upstairs bedrooms, baths, and linen closets. (I have to change into my costume *somewhere*.) Well, my story. I walked one day into this mansion and came face-to-face with an aquarium, the size of a picture window, set right into the wall. I mean there were no wires or filters or motors. Just a glass wall behind which there swam the most exotic fish you ever saw outside a National Geographic. It was breathtaking! The tank also had an automatic feeder, and the hostess had not counted on the commotion this would cause! Twenty minutes into my "romance," that automatic feeder dispensed dinner! The tank became a kaleidoscope of color! It was a rainbow come to life, as those beautiful fish began to swish from behind rock formations and water ferns to swim toward those tiny particles of floating food! For once my book was second-best entertainment, even for me! We took an intermission! For a few magic minutes we were mermaids in the South seas! That's romance you can't read!

And there is nothing more gracious than a grandfather clock! It gives an unmistakable grandeur standing there so solidly, chiming away no matter what. It gives you a sense of security! "Some things never change," it seems to say. "Chime, chime, chime."

They can also give you a headache. Giving a dramatic review in the same house with a grandfather clock is like doing Macbeth under Big Ben! Just as you get the group in the palm of your hand, the quarter hour rolls around! Ding, ding! Everybody looks at a watch. They look out the window. They look back at you. Another fifteen minutes. Then, just as you have them again, the half hour comes up! DING, ding, ding, ding, DING! Oh, well, such a sense of history!

A clock doesn't have to be BIG, actually, to play havoc with your plans. I remember one palatial house where the people were world travelers. Each room had furnishings from a different country. The living room resembled its counterpart in a chalet in the Alps. On the mantle was the most charming little cuckoo clock from Switzerland! I was doing a very serious review that day, something about China and the Boxer Rebellion, I think, and every fifteen minutes that bird came out of that clock and said, "Cuckoo! Cuckoo! Cuckoo!" It was hilarious, at least.

But the clock I remember most was a wristwatch! I was to entertain at a lovely, large Christmas dinner given by Dr. and Mrs. Edmund Lacy, of the Dallas Baptist College faculty. Mrs. Lacy's uncle was there for the season, and I was excited to meet him. He was the renowned Dr. W. R. White, for so long the president of Baylor University. Dr. White, though retired for many years by that time, was still wise and wonderful and was the life of the party, until I started to tell my Christmas stories. He was seated in a soft easy chair on the front row, and soon he went to sleep! It was past his bedtime, and he had probably heard all my stories! About midway through my program, we heard a tiny chime, like a silver dinner bell in a doll house. Suddenly Dr. White's head bobbed. His eyes opened wide. With a wink, he pulled back his wide French cuffs to reveal a wristwatch, alarming! He snapped off the little alarm and whispered loudly to the lady next to him, "Time for my pill!" Whereupon he took a tiny pillbox out of his vest pocket, put a pill under his tongue, smiled contentedly at the lady next to him and at me! I never missed a word, and Dr. White was awake for the rest of the night! He has forgotten more information than I'll ever know. But he won't forget the *time* because he has a watch that will tell him!

Let me hasten to say that I am relating the exceptions rather than the rule! Most reviews go really well, and the vast majority of hostesses are marvelous. They take pets to the vet.

They cut out piped-in music. They unplug telephones. One woman even disconnected her doorbell. (Well, she *did* have an unusual doorbell. It played "Mine Eyes Have Seen the Glory"!) And most hostesses stop clocks (or put them under pillows). Only a handful of times each year do we have such hilarity as I have mentioned! But it does prove "The Perils Of a Public Speaker."

Actually, houses have fewer "pitfalls" than country clubs! I could write another BOOK about busybody waitresses, loud buffet lines, and intercoms that go, "Yellow Buick, license XYZ-6824, left your lights on"! There's also *always* a lawn mower or a tree trimmer somewhere on the grounds. And once they laid carpet in the ballroom above me! There is a country club in Dallas that has an ice maker that can be heard all over the building, and another with a four-tiered fountain in the foyer. When your meeting is in the main dining room, it's like performing by Niagara Falls. But the absolute BEST can-you-top-this was the day an accordion curtain was pulled across the middle of a banquet room and a club was put at each end, supposedly both in "private rooms." On one side of the curtain I was doing an action-adventure tale about an oil tanker in the Persian Gulf. On the other side of the curtain, twenty singers and a grand piano were doing a salute to Cole Porter! I'll let you guess who had the last word!

And there is at least *one* country club in town that would like to ban *me*. They have a large bowl of little green mints in the lobby on a table covered with a green velvet cloth. There are always fresh flowers on the table too. It is a beautiful arrangement. One day as I was leaving the club with some ladies who had just heard me speak, I took several of the green mints and commented, "These are the best mints in town! I wish I had a bag full!" A *year later* that same group gathered at the same club, and as we were leaving, one darling little lady came up to me. "I remember how you love those mints, Dearie," she said, "and so today I brought a plastic bag from home!" Whereupon she pulled out of her purse a self-closing refrigerator bag bulging with mints! She must have emptied the whole bowl into her bag! She presented it to me proudly. To return the mints at that point would have hurt her terribly. I smiled weakly and accepted my present, praying that the manager was out to lunch, out for coffee, or at the very least *out* of the *lobby*. I left, hurriedly, with my costume, my book, and a plastic bag full of ill-gotten gain!

And then there are my continual brushes with the law. I am as close to perfect as you can come (of course, my tongue is in my cheek), but I have one flaw, at least. I exceed the speed limit. Not excessively, you understand. I go just a *little* over the limit. Part of it is because I'm in a hurry. Part of it is because I'm thinking about what I'm going to say when I get there instead of thinking about *getting* there. Anyway, I speed a little. I will also drive around two blocks to get by STOP signs. I *know* they are there for my safety, and I obey them, but they bother me! I have never hurt a soul, including myself. (I *have* dented a few fenders. I have backed into iron railings at playgrounds. And one time I sideswiped a parking meter.) But I do sometimes exceed the speed limit a little, and the police are on to me. They follow me around. I have a collection of traffic tickets to prove it!

We have a friend named John who is a perfectly respectable lawyer. He does not *have* to spend his time in traffic court. But for me he does, saying things like, "But, Sir, she *says* she STOPPED." When I pass the white marble Dallas County Courthouse, on top of which sits the jail, I say, "There but for the grace of John, go I!" I have tried to be law-abiding. I *am* better.

But once I almost ended up in court on a drunk-driving charge! At first, it wasn't funny. It was the dead of winter. No snow or ice, just bone-chilling COLD. I had been coughing for about two weeks, night and day. Each review was worse. My voice became weaker and weaker, and once, in the middle of my "romance," I had to leave the room and cough for about five minutes. Christmas was coming, however, and I knew there would be about two weeks when I could coddle myself, so I hoped to fill my last few engagements. My last engagement before Christmas was still to come, a woman's club in a small city about an hour's drive from Dallas. I felt I had to do it. They were counting on me. They had made decorations. I *wanted* to do it.

All week long I had survived on hot tea with honey, the more heat and honey the better. So on the morning I was to speak, I filled a huge thermos with hot honey-tea and took to the road. The review went surprisingly well. The woman's club looked like a Christmas card. The mike was good, and I didn't cough once! I was halfway home, relieved to be alive, when I was suddenly hit with a spasm of coughing to end all spasms! I was convulsed. I couldn't see. I couldn't catch my breath. I jammed on the brakes and jerked the car onto the median (there being no shoulder on either side of the highway at that particular point). I fell over on the front seat coughing and gasping and gagging and reached for my thermos.

Suddenly sirens wailed! Lights flashed! Two highway patrolmen came running! They were beating on the windows, their breath making little clouds of steam. I raised up, bleary and bloodshot, clutching my thermos to me!

"Lady," the big one yelled, "Do you realize you have just endangered the lives of a lot of people? You have been weaving down the road for four miles, and then you cut across two lanes and land on the median. What in the world is wrong with you? And *what* have you got in that thermos?"

"Hot *tea*," I gasped, but he couldn't hear me. Actually my vocal chords were dead, and I wasn't making any sound. Then, with do-or-die inspiration, I thrust the thermos out the window. "Have some," I mouthed. "Please, have some!"

He unscrewed the cap. He scowled. He smelled. He looked incredulous. "That's hot *tea!*"

I nodded vigorously, and mouthed, "With honey! Have some!" Then I started to cough again. I was convulsed. I couldn't see. I couldn't catch my breath. Suddenly, that was the most concerned patrolman you ever saw. He poured tea into the thermos top and held it in the window to my mouth. I think he burned his hand. After a minute, my vocal chords came to. "There're some paper cups in the pocket," I managed.

Well, maybe it was because they were so cold. Maybe it was because it was Christmas. But I poured with all the graciousness of a matron at her silver service, and those two patrolmen sipped daintily from their paper cups. They seemed grateful, and one of them asked for the ingredients. And I shall always remember those two men who shared with me a spot of tea in the middle of a modern highway that led home for the holidays!

How could I forget? They gave me a ticket!

3
Planes, Trains, and Pony Express

I remember how excited I was to see Omaha, Nebraska, specifically the Strategic Air Command! The very name sounds of red-white-and-blue assurance! Somehow down deep in my heart I've always known that whether war, plague, or pestilence, SAC would save me! Now I was to see! I was to speak to perhaps the most prestigious Officers Wives Club in the country, almost a thousand members, and my program was a light study of the life and style of Agatha Christie called "Make Mine Murder," which was always fun to do! I looked forward to the day.

My plane arrived in Omaha at nearly midnight. I was met by the program chairman and the president of the Officers Wives Club, both bright young women and both wives of colonels. The program chairman was a beautiful Italian with a name to match. It sounded something like "Coca-Cola." She read my mind. "It sounds like Coca-Cola, doesn't it," she laughed! We were friends from the first! We skimmed through the city, passing the Mutual of Omaha building and several other "sights," and were soon at a motel where I was to stay. We were chitchating away, in a laughing, lighthearted mood as we entered my room and suddenly received something of a surprise. On the bar was a sample of every kind of liquor sold in the hotel! "Mercy," I said, "we must be in the wrong room! Surely this is reserved for some general who is planning a party!"

The desk clerk was called. I informed him, "There are setups here for a party of twenty people!" (To the side I heard Coca-Cola mutter under her breath, "Or a bash for ten!") A very efficient voice on the telephone told me, "There is no mistake, ma'am. We furnish all rooms with refreshment! Your hostess will pay only for what you drink!"

It was so late and the day had been so long for all of us that everything seemed hilarious! I announced to my host-esses, "You are going to save some money *tonight!*" And we fell onto the bed giggling like school girls.

"This is something last year's program chairman didn't *tell* me," wailed Coca-Cola! "When you have a Southern Baptist from Texas coming in, get the *liquor* out of the *room!*"

Mornings in Omaha can be brilliant, and the morning after I arrived was! The Officers Club was spit-and-polish perfect, and the tables in the banquet room were heaped with flowers and food. To my left, at luncheon, was Mrs. Leavitt, wife of General Lloyd Leavitt, one of the commanders of SAC. She could not have been more warm and welcoming. During lunch she said, "Perhaps you would like to see my home and our command post!" I was overwhelmed! Of course I would like to see everything! Quickly I went to a telephone and changed my flight to Dallas from early afternoon to early evening!

The review was well received, but by then the review was *not* the most important moment of my day! After lunch I went with Mrs. Leavitt to General's Row where the "Quarters" were built almost one hundred years ago and look like pictures on the pages of a history book. The "Quarters" of

General and Mrs. Leavitt was a marvelous old mansion with wonderful wood floors, winding stairs and three stories, all furnished appropriately with antiques. It was like being back in a time of white gloves and gallantry, cotillions, and two o'clock teas! Any lady would have loved living in that house!

From General's Row we went, with military escort, to a large, plain-looking office building several stories tall. Believe me, that building is anything but plain, for beneath it lies the absolute center of the United States defensive military management! "Peace is our profession," the brass plaque reads, and here they practice defensive military exactly as I practice defensive medicine, "An ounce of prevention is worth a pound of cure"! Down a hallway there is a door marked, "No Lone Zone." Beyond that door not even a general can be alone but must have military escort. And then we were walking down a sloping corridor. I have forgotten how many feet, forty or fifty feet, down into the dark of the earth before we came to the Command Post. It is like a theater. There is a large "auditorium," the floor of which is filled with computers of every size and shape, little lights flashing and racing and tracing! My escort and I entered a balcony above. There is one long curving desk and a line of large leather chairs, each one assigned to a general. I was invited to sit in the commander's chair to view the operations in the theater. As I sat down I saw just to my left THE TELEPHONE. I was surprised to see that it was yellow, instead of red! Then I saw clearly six screens the size of movie screens raised around the theater, each one showing a different place around the world. The scenes on the screens changed constantly, as the world changed. As I sat down I received the surprise of my life as I saw my name flashed across the center screen: "Welcome, Joy Davis!" If never, ever again in my life I am a Very Important Person, I was at that moment! I wanted to wave at the men below to let them see my delight, but I was too timid to lift my hand, and they did not so much as look up. They were too busy keeping track of the whole world. For the next thirty minutes, I received a comprehensive course in SURVIVAL! I was afraid to ask questions, afraid I would say something really dumb like, "Where's Europe?" But I did manage, "Do the Russians know we have all this?!"

"I certainly hope so," my escort replied dryly and continued with my tour. A huge map flashed on one screen. "These are the locations of SAC around the world," he said. "We'll talk to whichever one you want." I pointed, somewhere in the Aleutians, I think, and momentarily that base was on the line, giving me the report of the battle-ready conditions for that day. "And now we'll talk to Looking Glass," he told me. This, I think, was the biggest thrill of all. The Looking Glass is a continually flying command post, a plane outfitted with its own computers and team of military men. Should Omaha be blown away, at least all our battle plans and several commanders will be safe in the air to fly to Washington or to carry on the war from the air if there is no way to do it from the ground. There are two planes called Looking Glass. They alternate every eight hours with a fresh team of masterminds aboard. The pilot, who has two perfectly good eyes, flies with one eye covered with a black eye patch. An aerial nuclear blast would blind him. If that happens, he will simply move the eye patch to cover his blinded eye and continue to fly. The safety of remaining America would depend on him and his passengers!

Returning to the "real world" above, I felt like Alice in Wonderland, stepping back through the "looking glass" to a place where everything is right! But just in case someday, somewhere, somehow, it all goes wrong, there are some men in Omaha at a place called SAC who will save as much of

America as possible! I've put them on my prayer list, right up there with my *life*!

Outside two colonels and their wives were waiting to take me to dinner at the Officer's Club and then to deliver me to my plane! It was, indeed, a special day for a "popular public speaker"!

There *are* days, however, that are memorable only for their confusion and frustration! Some days your energies are *gone* before you get where you are going! I had such a day in Des Moines!

I was supposed to speak to the Des Moines Woman's Club. It was a day in November, a luncheon at noon, followed by my performance. I was anxious to see the famed old Sherman House, which is the home of the woman's club in Des Moines. It had been built by the brother of the Civil War general and now stood in gracious grandeur as the home of the woman's club. Many music recitals and art functions were held in the lovely, large auditorium that had been added to the mansion. According to the airlines, it would be a one day's journey only. Lovely. Everything in order.

The day dawned and by 5:30 AM I was on my way to DFW airport. I had only a cup of tea in my tummy since my flight was to be a breakfast flight. I was dressed warmly, high-heeled boots, plaid wool skirt, cashmere sweater, and velvet blazer. Perfect for football, but certainly not for an appearance at the woman's club. I carried two large bags, one containing fourteen posters and four books, the other a costume, a luncheon dress, and extra shoes for each. These two bags I checked and carried with me only my makeup bag, which also held my extra hair! I would be in Kansas City in an hour, having been fed breakfast in flight. Then I would catch another plane and be in Des Moines in forty minutes, by midmorning. This would give me two hours time to get to the woman's club, set up my props and posters, don my luncheon dress, and greet my ladies at noon looking lovely! But! Leaving Dallas proved to be a problem.

At 6:30 AM, as we were walking down the ramp into the plane, a crash like a collision of space ships shook the ramp! Unbalanced, we rushed back up the ramp. A huge piece of machinery had toppled from one of the movable maintenance towers onto the nose cone of our plane. It was crushed and leaking some sort of liquid! Obviously we were not going any place in *that* plane.

Hurriedly we were rerouted, this time through Oklahoma City and Wichita, Kansas. I would now reach Kansas City late morning, barely in time for a connection that would land in Des Moines at noon. This was much too close for comfort, but there were no more choices to be made. At Oklahoma City I had ten minutes time on the ground. I dashed to the phone to call my program chairman in Des Moines. No answer. She had undoubtedly left for the airport, thinking I would be landing in a matter of minutes. (There had been no time to call her from DFW in Dallas. The "new" flight was holding its doors open for all the dislodged passengers.) So praying that she would not have a heart attack (program chairmen are prone to heart attacks and understandably so), I returned to the plane. When the flight attendant offered me coffee, I realized I had not been fed breakfast. Breakfast was back in Dallas with a damaged nose cone.

Kansas City looked bleak as we circled the city. Never one to be silent in any situation, I commented to the young man beside me, "I do so hope we are in time for the connecting flight! I *must* reach Des Moines by 1 PM."

"Well," he said cheerfully, "I *live* in K.C., and the airport here is not known for its convenience. But don't worry. There are lots of little private plane services. You might charter something, I mean if you really *must* get there!"

I laughed. I thought he was jesting!

On the ground in Kansas City, I knew he was not. I experienced one of my rare moments of pure panic when a smiling ticket agent told me that my connecting flight had propeller problems and had never left Houston. It would not arrive in K.C. until midafternoon. There was no other flight to Des Moines. They could not even get me back to Dallas until evening. It was now too late to *drive* to Des Moines. So sorry!

I gasped, "So sorry? You're so sorry?" Suddenly I remembered the young man who sat beside me a few minutes before. I gathered myself together and tried to sound calm and casual as if I did this sort of thing all the time, "Where", I said, "can I charter a plane?"

The ticket agent did not move a muscle. "I'm sure I don't know," he said helpfully.

"But surely you know some names of air services, some number I can call!"

"Look in the yellow pages," he suggested with half his heart and walked away.

I ran to a phone booth and looked frantically among the unfamiliar names. I called one. "Lady," said the man, "all our planes are in the air taking people to places they couldn't get to *yesterday*! Good luck!"

Three more phone calls, and I finally found an air service with an available plane. I asked the cost and held my breath, $277.00! If I had continued on the commercial flight the forty minutes would have cost me $30.00. "I'll call you back," I said. I sat in the phone booth trying to make a decision of some sort. Nobody would blame me if I didn't get to Des Moines. Crushed nose cones could not ever be classified as my fault! On the other hand, there were several hundred women in Des Moines who were dressing for lunch even at this very moment, and one program chairman who was having a heart attack. So what if I went home with $277.00 less? I surely wouldn't make a penny sitting in a phone booth in Kansas City! I called the air service. "Come get me," I said, "and hurry, Honey!" Too late I remembered I wasn't in the South. "Honey" said he was on his way!

My next move was to dash to a page phone. "Please announce that a private plane has been chartered for Des Moines and that anyone wishing to share expenses should meet me at Gate 7!"

A monotone over the telephone said, "We can't do that, ma'am."

"Why in heaven's name not?" I shouted.

"We are not in the business of chartering planes for passengers!"

"Of *course* you are not," I screamed. "*I* have chartered the plane, and *I* want somebody to help me with expenses. Say it's a *private* plane!"

"We can't do that, ma'am."

By now I am jumping up and down, getting louder and louder, and people in the lobby are looking at me! "You most certainly *can* do that," I declared. "Your airline has left me here without any alternatives, and I am trying desperately to salvage the situation. I am going to let a lot of people down (not to mention lose a lot of money) if I don't get to Des Moines by one o'clock! The *least* you can do is make my announcement, or I am going to go to the airport manager!"

It occurred to me later that it was probably the airport manager who had made the rule in the first place, but at the time it sounded like a good thing to say. The monotone on the telephone finally agreed to make the announcement, once!

Within minutes several businessmen were converging on

Gate 7, briefcases flying, looking for the lady who had chartered a plane. They flipped a coin. A good-looking Jewish boy won the toss to be my companion. That is, I *thought* he was a boy. He introduced himself. He had a Master degree in business management and was the vice-president of a plastics manufacturing firm. *Good Grief,* I thought, *the vice-presidents of the world are getting younger.* We ran together out to the tiny plane that was taxiing toward us.

"Look," I said to him, "they have lost my luggage, my clothes, my props and my posters, but at least I have my extra eyelashes and hair with me. Can you hold a mirror?"

And so for the next forty minutes, somewhere in time between Kansas City and Des Moines, I gave one unbelieving Jewish young man a lesson in ladies' cosmetics. "I am *amazed,*" he kept saying. "You *do* look *different!*"

Des Moines materialized below us. The pilot had radioed ahead to the private airport, which had called the woman's club. The program chairman had delayed her heart attack long enough to leap into her car and speed out to meet me. Her motor was running as we landed, and I raced for her car. We sped back through the city, ignoring traffic lanes and lights. The woman's club loomed ahead of us, and we careened around to the stage door. Several hundred ladies had finished lunch and filled the auditorium. The president was presiding with one eye on the wings! My arrival at the stage door was met with a collective sigh of relief from six board members! It was 1:15 PM, and my introduction was a bit brief.

I had been up since 4:30 AM. I had not had breakfast. I had not had lunch. I was dressed for a football game. But that is the only time in my life I have gotten an ovation just for walking out on stage!

The review went . . . well, actually I've often wondered *how* it went. You'd have to ask them. I didn't forget any lines, but surely the performance was less than it could have been with costume, props, and posters. Everyone was wonderful afterward. The program chairman took me to the kitchen where they found for me some salad and finger sandwiches. We walked through the lovely old house, surely one of the most beautiful homes of its era, and then left for the airport. We had a watchful eye on the weather. A blizzard was due to blow in at any moment. By then I could think of nothing worse than to be snowbound in Iowa. But it was not to be! With relief I took off for Kansas City.

Arriving in Kansas City, I found that my bags had caught up with me. There was a lot of discussion at the counter about refunding my $30.00 for the flight that should have taken me to Des Moines that morning. When it was finished, I turned to find a handsomely dressed man standing near me. "Sounds like you've had a hard day," he said, "why don't we have dinner here in Kansas City. You can take a later flight back to Dallas!" Well, it had been twenty-five years since anybody had asked me for a date. Is this what they call a pickup, I wondered? I looked puzzled. It *had* been a hard day. The hair was wild, the makeup a mess, and the body was sagging. It couldn't have been my beauty that had dazzled him. Then I realized, he had overheard the conversation at the counter about the private plane. He thought I was RICH! I laughed, a little too loudly, "I have to get home to my husband," I said and walked away, waving to him with my boarding pass! Now it was *he* who looked puzzled.

Sinking wearily into my window seat, I sighed. Surely it was over. My bags and I were on the way home, and now nothing else would happen! Wrong! It happened. Dinner was served. Turkey and dressing and all the trimmings. I ate, famished, having had nothing all day but salad and finger sandwiches. I was just settling down for a few winks before

Dallas when the plane hit an air pocket! Then there was thunder and lightning and rain on the window! Literally, during our last descent into Dallas, we had hit an electrical storm, and that plane tossed and turned and churned as if on the open sea. My turkey and dressing and all the trimmings were suddenly confused, whether to go down or up. Gratefully we were on the ground in a few minutes, and my dinner decided to stay down!

Seventeen hours after leaving home I was back! Jewell gathered me in out of the thunder and lightning and led me to the bed. He unzipped my boots and shook the rain off my blazer.

"You are losing an eyelash," he observed.

"Wake me in the morning," I murmured. "I have to entertain the garden club at ten o'clock!"

4
A Calling, Not a Career

I used to think I had a career. Well, at first a hobby. You can't call it a career when you speak to the PTA on Founder's Day for fifteen dollars! But then there was the DAR and the UDC and the ladies of the Lions Club. And then there were the book clubs, the garden clubs, and the women's clubs, and more churches than I could accept. And *then* I decided it was not a hobby anymore. I could call it a career. Not a *big* career, a *little* career then. But each month there was a bit more money, and when I bought a couch and a chair to match, with my own money, I decided it was definite! I had a career! It was fun, and I felt important! Thirty clubs a year seemed like a lot then! Now I do one hundred and thirty. It's still fun, and I still feel important. But! I don't call it a career anymore!

From the first I loved to do the Christian novels for church women. It was in church that I began to be a "public speaker," and most of my programs were for Christian gatherings. So when I began to be asked by secular clubs, I wondered what I would want to do for these groups. Bestsellers are not always the best *books*, and some of the better ones are not suited for drama. Biography and autobiography are interesting if the subject is interesting, but these are not "romantic." It's like looking for a needle in a haystack to find a good story. How would I approach my appearances before secular clubs? Surely I could never do a Christian novel. Or could I?

It was close to the Easter season when one of the most social groups in the city, the Dallas Country Club, called for a performance at Ladies Day. It was only my second season to review in Dallas, and I was so excited! I wanted so much to make a great impression.

At the same time I was preparing a program for a Christian woman's club to celebrate the Easter season. I had found a beautiful book by Frank G. Slaughter called *The Thorn of Arimathea*. It was based on the legend that Joseph of Arimathea was the believer who took the gospel to the "bright isle of Britannia" before it was ever England. Also the love legend of Veronica and Quintus was woven romantically through the tale. The setting for this historical story was soon after the resurrection of Christ. I had done some research and collected a lot of history on the other disciples and the roads they took after the resurrection, thus effectively spreading the gospel far and wide around the world. I wanted to correlate this with our lives as Christians, especially at the Easter season, as *we* spread the gospel wherever we go! Also! I had a terrific toga! It made me look something like the figures on old Roman fountains!

For the Dallas Country Club, the more I read the more I rejected. I found some exciting secular novels, but somehow nothing seemed to fit. I prayed. It was important to my new "career" to do well at the country club. All those women belonged to other groups and organizations. I wanted to entertain them, but how, in heaven's name?! They had all been around the world. They had all been entertained by the best, from Broadway to Vienna. What would possibly please them?

As I prayed daily, the idea presented itself to me that I should do the same book for the ladies of the country club as for the ladies of the Christian women's club. It seemed completely improbable to me that the same program would do. The ladies at the country club would be coming prepared for a light program, a luncheon, laughter. Yet the more I prayed, the more I was convinced that I should do the Christian book at the country club. Actually, by this time, I had no choice. I had not found another novel.

The day of the program at the country club found me filled with apprehension. Why on earth wasn't I doing scenes from *Sound of Music*? What in the world was I thinking of, doing *The Thorn of Arimathea*? This wasn't church. It was a ladies spring luncheon.

I entered the room in my Roman toga and began the book. Soon the tale of romance took over, and I forgot to be afraid. The story is one of faith in Christ as living Lord. It tells of the dedication to the death of his followers, as they leave the land of the Mediterranean Sea to tell of the Man who walked with them there. At the end, the lovers, who have been separated, find one another again in a garden where blooms the flowering thorn bush from Arimathea. It is a marvelous moment!

I finished the book and bowed. At first there was not a sound. It was as if time held back its breath. And then there was thunderous applause ringing through the room! Relieved, I raised my head and was startled to see that they were standing, all around the room! I bowed again and again!

And it was there, on that stage that day, that I thought, *Lord! I don't have a mere career! I have a calling! If I can tell the story of Jesus, anywhere, anytime, and get a response like this, then you must have meant for me to be a "special" kind of public speaker! This must be my commission! It is no longer simply my pleasure. It is your plan!*

Since that day I have seen God's hand a hundred times as he has led me to the right places, at the right times, with the right books. I do not mean to say that I always do Christian programs. Certainly, I review secular books, best-sellers, and popular plays. But always there is a way to weave a Christian comment into some part of the program, a word here, a thought there, a sentence somewhere else. And I have a book full of beautiful notes from women who have remembered that word, or that thought, and been moved enough to thank me for the lift it gave their lives!

That's what the Lord can do! Lift you from dark to light, from sadness to gladness, from confusion and fear to peace! And that's what I tell the world! It's my witness! It's my joyful, joyful noise!

Sometimes I make the mistake of worrying about conditions I can't control, like the weather. And I worry about the acoustics in auditoriums, the mikes, and the clatter of kitchens in country clubs. I used to worry most of all about churches: Would there be children in the audience? Would the choir go to sleep? Would the announcements take thirty minutes of my time? After fifteen years on my feet in front of people I *think* I am through with worrying. I'd like to be. I'm learning!

I remember recently preparing for the state convention for Christian Multimedia and Communications. A lot of church librarians were going to be there, and I was to present something at the luncheon on the last day. I wanted to do it, but I was not satisfied with the surroundings. The schedule was going to be tight. My time was to be a fast forty minutes instead of the sixty I usually have. People were bound to be getting up and down and going in and out during the lunch. It would never do! I stewed and stewed over my typewriter. At last my daughter drew the line, "Mom," she said exasperated, "Will you *stop*! Remember, it's not *your* program! It's *God's*!"

Well, why didn't I think of that?! Of course. It was God's program. And he could see to the schedule and the time and the mikes and the movement of the people. All I had to do was to prepare. (I am happy to tell you that he worked it out beautifully, and it was one of the best times I've ever had!)

Indeed, God has cared for me *many* times, but none so notable as a day in Wichita Falls, Texas! I was to perform for Baptist Women's Day at the First Baptist Church of Wichita Falls. It was a Monday in May, which was memorable because it was the beginning of the week in which Drew Ann would graduate from high school.

Three weeks before, Jewell had left Dallas for what was to be a brief business trip to Athens, Greece. He had looked forward to some sight-seeing, as well as his meetings with officials of the Greek Air Force in the Hellanic Headquarters, the equivalent of the Pentagon. He would be home well before graduation! So he said! His time in Athens proved as profitable as he had hoped. He was able to see something of the country and to collect some beautiful pieces in brass and onyx to bring home. Indeed, all went well until the last day! That was the day that the Greek National Labor Union decided to disagree with the government! Well and good, except that in Greece they don't do it at the conference table. They do it with tanks and guns and tear gas! Jewell left his last meeting to find the laborites "demonstrating" on the street directly in front of his hotel. Besides the tanks and guns and tear gas, they had built bonfires at each intersection. Just outside the hotel, Jewell salvaged an unexploded tear gas cannister from one of the fires. (Just a little something extra to bring home, along with the onyx and brass.) And for the next half hour he took pictures of the "war" from his window.

It was Friday, before graduation on the *next* Friday, that the office called me. There was a little disturbance in Greece, they said. Everybody was on strike and the airport was closed. Maybe Jewell would be home, and maybe he wouldn't. Oh, wonderful.

That same Friday morning Drew Ann had left for her senior luncheon. We were to meet later at a mother-daughter tea. Before she left she put about $400.00 worth of clothes (including several new things she had bought for Senior Week) into the washer. I was to transfer them from the washer to the dryer. When I went to do so, I found to my monumental dismay that she had left a ball-point pen in one of the pockets. Every piece of $400.00 worth of clothes was streaked with ink! I threw them wet into the tub and left for the tea. We met. She said cheerfully, "Hi, Mom! And what have *you* done all day?"

I replied, "Your father is in a war, and there was a ball-point pen in your pocket!"

All day Saturday I worked over the clothes. Most I saved. Others, the cleaners eventually saved. Only one or two pieces were a total loss. But I had *planned* to spend Saturday on the preparation of the small part I had in the service on Baccalaureate Sunday. It was only a small segment of the service, a poem and a "word of wisdom," but it was Drew Ann's baccalaureate, and I wanted it to be perfect. Finally, about 10 PM, I finished the last of the clothes and leaped into the tub myself. Surely I could collect my thoughts now and be through by midnight.

It was then that I discovered the first and only lump I

have ever found on my body. It was small, high up on the inside of my left leg, and it was definitely new. I froze, a rather natural reaction to all we have read about "lumps." I assessed my situation. It was late Saturday night. The next day was Baccalaureate Sunday. And Monday morning I had to drive to Wichita Falls for Baptist Women's Day. It would be Tuesday before I could see my doctor. That was that. I prayed that I would not worry more than necessary. It was important that I keep my peace. By midnight I had decided what to say in the service Sunday, and I went to bed and to sleep. I remember reading Psalms 127:2: "It is vain for you to rise up early, or sit up late, to eat the bread of sorrows: for so he giveth his beloved sleep!"

The Sunday morning baccalaureate was beautiful. There was such excitement, and I did not want to worry Drew Ann. I held together for her, and my part on the program was perfect.

But Monday morning was a different matter. I awakened in the wee dark hours before dawn, tossing and turning. The worry of the last three days suddenly seemed overwhelming. I felt a floodtide of sorrow. My husband was in Greece in the middle of a "disturbance." My daughter's new clothes were in doubtful condition. And high up on my left leg there was a lump, which could mean nothing at all, or it could mean my life. At the moment I was inclined to believe the latter. Also, I was terribly, terribly tired.

I began to cry. I cried hard and long and loudly for hours. (That was, of course, way back when I could cry and get away with it. You remember, when you could cry and then wash the face, blow the nose, and nobody was the wiser?! Those days are long gone. The price I pay now for a good cry is puffy, purple circles under both eyes and a swollen red nose in between. Reminds you of Rudolf in middle age.) But way back then I could cry and not look like I had cried, and so I did.

At daylight I made tea and toast. It was almost time to leave for Wichita Falls. I could barely contain my tears, much less remember my lines. "Lord," I prayed, "this is your day. It must be because it surely isn't mine! There are several hundred women waiting for me. They deserve your best blessing. If *you* don't do it today, Lord, it won't get done. I'm lost and alone and too tired to think. Show me thy rod and thy staff, Lord! I have to lean on *some*thing!"

When I reached Wichita Falls and found the church, the first thing I saw was a packed parking lot. Ladies were walking from blocks away. Inside they were hurriedly setting up tables in the hallway. Reservations for the luncheon were long since sold out, and the large dining room was overflowing. Women without reservations were to be seated in the hallway. "We'll feed them till the food runs out," said the hostess, bustling about. In the foyer I saw a poster, a darling paper doll, with my face, in a blue hoop skirt, identical to my costume for the day. Some committee member had been creative! I went into the bride's room and began to dress.

I can't tell you how it happened. I'll never know, but suddenly out on the stage my story came alive! Admittedly, I had good material. I was reviewing a book by Eugenia Price, *The Beloved Invader* (New York: Harper & Row, 1965), about a man who became a legend in his lifetime on Saint Simons Island, Georgia. He was a romantic man, who loved devotedly. He was devastated by the loss of his wife and his son, both to untimely, accidental death. But this man, a minister, believed in the goodness of God, and his power to redeem all of life and death.

"God is not only the redeemer of our sin," he preached, "but of our circumstance as well. He will not waste a single problem, a single hurt or heartache, a single tear. Our God is a redeemer God, and He stands minute by minute before us, inviting us to let *Him* have the sorrow, let *Him* have the pain, let *Him* have the disappointment, . . . to trust Him to make something useful, something creative, out of every tragedy that darkens our lives!" (p. 256).

This man did not waste his own great grief. He *used* it, creatively, and opened his large, lovely house as a home for orphaned boys, in memory of his own little loved one. For half a century the Anson Dodge Home for Boys cared for those who were lost and lonely, without father and mother, and shared with them a faith, as well as food and clothes and shelter. That happened because one man allowed the Lord to make redemptive use of his entire life, thus turning his tragedies into triumphs!

When I was finished the women were weeping. There was a sweet spirit in that place, like love and peace and complete trust. Afterwards women came to me to tell me their testimonies of faith and fortitude. There were many tears. And one woman, her face washed with her weeping yet radiant, told me, "Only a few months ago I buried my only boy. This book has given me the first light I have seen since that day! Thank God!"

Driving home through the dusk I was serene, rested, settled in my soul. Tomorrow would be with God, as today had been!

On Tuesday morning my doctor insisted on seeing me immediately. I was with him for only a few minutes. "A harmless cyst," he smiled. "It will go away soon!" And it did.

On Wednesday morning my husband's office called. The Athens airport was open. All Greek flights were full, but there was a TWA Tourist Charter that would leave early Thursday and land at DFW late Thursday, twenty hours before graduation. Jewell would be on it!

The following Friday night, as we sat with other proud parents watching our children take that "milestone step," I remembered Monday morning. I remembered the tears in the dark hours before dawn and the worry and the weariness. I remembered my fear and confusion. And then I remembered a little later the light on a woman's face and the sweet spirit in that place. And I remembered something more: the peace had come to me *before* I knew the answers. The security had come *before* I was safe! I felt like singing, "Whatever my lot, thou hast taught me to say, It is well, it is well with my soul!" Ah, Lord. "Thy rod and Thy staff," how they comfort me!

The greatest test of faith always comes when we cannot see an immediate sign that God is in command. Often it looks like the Lord has taken a holiday. We leave messages at the throne of grace, but he doesn't get back to us, for awhile. It has happened to me more than once!

One summer, early in the '70s, I was asked to teach two classes in Christian drama during Recreation Week at Glorieta, a beautiful Baptist conference center in New Mexico. Another Baptist conference center in Ridgecrest, North Carolina, had been like a summer retreat to me since I grew up east of the Mississippi River. But Glorieta, being west of the Mississippi River, was new to me, and I was anxious to see it. I drove out with my daughter and my mother. My husband and son would join us in New Mexico. It was to be a fun, family week. I knew it would be a lot of work, but worthwhile.

Work, it was. There was not a minute of time for myself during the ten-hour days. I was tired, but happy; the adrenaline was high. I waited for Wednesday night with anticipation. This was the night that I would perform.

The program that I was to do was my favorite, for good

reason. I had never given it that I did not have a precious response. Called, "The Bible According to Broadway," it is a program in which I correlate the themes from Broadway with Bible truths. For instance, *Brigadoon* is the story of a fantasy town in Scotland that appears once every one hundred years, so the people in that town will remain the same, happy, healthy, and untouched by worldly wrong and trouble! People have always looked with longing for a "happy hunting ground," a Shangri-la, a Utopia, where for time and eternity they will find peace and pleasure. There *is* such a place, of course. Broadway calls it Brigadoon. The Christian calls it heaven!

There are other themes that I use from time to time with this program. The one I was to use at Glorieta correlates the lives of two women, the harlot of Spain, Dulcinea, who meets the man of La Mancha with his "impossible dream," and the harlot of Samaria, who meets the Man of Galilee! The program closes with a most moving characterization of the woman at the well and a strong statement of faith in the forgiveness of God. It is always a thrill for me to do this particular theme!

If I had known, however, what was to happen that Wednesday night, I would never have walked out on that stage. I was ready and waiting in the wings. Grady Nutt, the Christian humorist, was one of the program personalities that week and introduced me. It was Grady's idea to play several minutes of "mood music" before my performance to "set the theme." It had sounded like a good idea when Grady suggested it. That was the *last* time it sounded like a good idea. The audience did not interpret it as "mood music." They interpreted it as "intermission"!

People began to go out and in, to talk, to walk in the aisles. Before I reached the stage, four minutes later, I had lost the audience, and I never found them again! As I began to speak, I realized that the mike was not tuned properly. Grady had been using a stand mike. I was using a clip mike. The controls had not been tested or perhaps had not been turned from one mike to the other. Immediately I lost the attention of everyone who was not seated in the first fifteen rows. It was the most terrible thirty minutes of my life. When it was over I received polite applause. (Or I don't know, maybe it wasn't even polite. When there are 3,000 people, even *poor* applause can sound *polite*.) I left the stage and the auditorium and went to my room. I was numb, absolutely numb. I didn't begin to "feel" again until sometime around dawn.

It was then that the questions began. Where on earth was the Lord when I needed him?! Or perhaps this was a punishment. I repeated over and over again the phrase, "Pride goeth before destruction" (Prov. 16:18). Had I been too prideful?! I tried to see it as such a situation, but deep down in my heart I knew that this was not the problem. I have *always* given God the glory, and I have *always* known that without his help I would never get past the first paragraph. So then, if it weren't pride, perhaps I had not prayed enough. Perhaps I wasn't prepared spiritually. I had been so sure of myself and my material, and there had been no time for an "hour of power." Perhaps that was it.

The next morning I apologized to my drama class for the performance. "One should never attempt to share the Lord's message without spiritual preparation, as well as mental preparation," I said. The class was candid. Preparation or no preparation, they replied, the fact was that they couldn't *hear* me the night before. I was miserable.

For months I worried over that night at Glorieta. I wanted to find the fault in me or wherever. I would wake in the middle of the night and worry. I left messages with God, but he did not get back to me, then. Finally, eighteen months had gone by. I had almost forgotten about Glorieta. I wanted to put the disappointment in the past. What's done is done, and I couldn't dwell on it.

It was Christmas, and I was in the First Baptist Church of Lubbock, Texas, to do the life of Lottie Moon at the Sunday evening service. I had done this dramatization of the life of the missionary lady at the State WMU Convention in Abilene that fall, and the longtime minister of music at First Baptist in Lubbock, Ron Lowry, was one of the first to call to ask me to repeat the performance there one Sunday night in December. This was the night, and I was waiting in the choir room, while the members collected music and robes. The choir that night was made up almost entirely of college students from Texas Tech University. How like children they looked. Was I growing old and gray, I wondered?

Suddenly one of the young women came to my side. "I have just this minute realized who you are," she said! "I saw the announcement in this morning's bulletin about your program tonight, but I didn't recognize your name. Now that I see you, I remember! Aren't you the dramatist who did 'The Woman at the Well' at Glorieta two summers ago?!"

"Oh, dear," I wailed. "You remember . . ." I was prepared to be apologetic, but she went on with her words.

"Yes. Oh, yes, I remember! It was beautiful! I needed God's forgiveness that night! I had felt for a long, long time that I was failing him. I wanted my life to *amount* to *more* as a woman! It was wonderful to hear how he can touch you, and teach you to be a blessing for him! Like the Samaritan woman, I know I will *never be the same!*"

Hours passed. It was midnight before I reached my room and could savor what had been said. So! My professional performance had failed. That was an accepted fact. But I wondered now why I had worried. Somehow it suddenly seemed so insignificant, the fact that I had failed! For now I knew that the message of love and faith and forgiveness had reached out, over a mike that wouldn't work, over noise and restlessness, to the yearning heart of a young woman who needed God that night. She had been there, and God had been there, and they had found each other. Nothing else was necessary, certainly not my success or failure!

Our concern is not to be successful. Our only concern is to be *where* God wants us to be, doing *what* he wants us to do. Our efforts are effective, then, whether we see the results now or never! If it is his plan, or his program, all we have to do is carry it out. He will arrange the results, his way! It would be wonderful if we were always brilliant, beautiful, and wise. It would be wonderful if everything we attempted turned out well. But that will not always be. We must trust God to take what we give and make it good. For *that* is what turns any task, any lifetime, into a calling!

Don Miguel Cervantes, court poet of Spain in the 1600s, authored a masterful manuscript that is a standard work studied by college and graduate students of literature and language: *Don Quixote de La Mancha.*

Don Quixote is a timeless tale of a gentle old dreamer, an old man who is dedicated to ideals and who believes that nobility can be a way of life! The Don is a settled country gentleman, retired, who should be living his life in rest and contentment. But he becomes depressed at the decline of chivalry and "man's murderous ways toward man," and so he broods. At last the Don "lays down the melancholy burden of sanity, and conceives the strangest idea ever imagined in the mind of man." The old Don decides to disguise himself as a knight in shining armor and "sally forth" from his country estate to set to right all of the world's wrongs! Thus Cervantes created the memorable "man of la Mancha." The Broadway play *Man of La Mancha* was based on this book.

As the book begins we see the satire: how the old man does battle with a windmill, thinking it is a giant with four arms; how he follows the aimless shepherd's trail, insisting that this is "the road to glory"; how he has himself formally "knighted" by the innkeeper, wearing the barber's shaving mug for a helmet! The final irony is his meeting with the harlot, Aldonza. He places her on a pedestal of goodness and grace and calls her by another name, "Dulcinea."

The most poignant part of the book is about the relationship between Don Quixote, the little old man in the middle of a fantasy of knights and lords and ladies, and Aldonza, the young harlot who has known only the harsh ways of the world. Yet the old Don calls her his "lovely lady" and insists that she is all "goodness and grace." He promises to "follow the quest" in the precious name of "The Lady, Dulcinea."

At first Aldonza (Dulcinea) rejects Quixote rudely and roughly, for she trusts no man, but his gentle ways and gracious words leave her baffled and bewildered. She cries in her confusion and begs him to see her as she really is, as nothing, as no one! He replies plaintively that he sees only beauty and light and love! Finally, it is this unfounded but unfathomable belief in her basic goodness as a human being that has an emphatic effect upon this girl. By the end of the book, she has begun to see herself as *he* sees her, with a new direction, a new name, and a new way to walk! Don Quixote's "impossible dream" has become possible for Dulcinea!

There was, once, another woman, another harlot. We have come to call her the Samaritan woman at the well. The Samaritans were a race of half-breeds, a blend of Jewish blood and Assyrian blood, and they were an unclaimed class by both the pure Jew and the pure Assyrian. This particular Samaritan woman was also a harlot and was wounded constantly by her own people. She could not go to the well in the cool of the twilight time with the other women without hearing their curses of hatred for her, and so she chose to go at high noon, in the heat of the day, when she was assured of being alone!

One day, as she came walking to the well, she saw a Man.

He was clearly recognizable as a Galilean by the cut of the sandals. Immediately she was wary, as she was with all men, but as she came closer to him she saw that this Man was different from any other man. He would not seem as other men, she was sure; and he did not. He held out his hand toward the well, "Give me to drink" (John 4:7). And so she lowered her vessel into the clear, cool water, brought it up, and gave it to him, and he drank! He began to talk to her, then, about living water, about worship, prayer, and praise! Finally she cried, "Why do you talk to me? Why do you have anything at all to do with me? Don't you know who I am? A Samaritan! And . . . a . . . harlot!"

He looked at her with eyes of wisdom, "I know you. I know all about you. You've had many men and several husbands, and the man you have now is not your husband. But oh, I'm offering you a better way! A higher way! Faith! Hope! Love! And I'm offering you my *forgiveness*!"

You remember, don't you, that she believed! She ran into the village where before she'd been afraid to walk, and she pounded on the doors of the people! "Come with me to the well," she cried, "and see a Man Who told me everything I ever did and still forgave me!" And you remember, don't you, that they came to see for themselves and then stayed to listen and to learn as he told them of *his* impossible dreams! Love your fellowman as yourselves! Return good for evil! Peace on earth!

The Bible says that many believed! A whole town had been turned toward God! And who did he use as his witness? A sinful, Samaritan woman! A woman who recognized her need and wanted living water! A woman who cared that others should come to him too!

Oh! The wonder of it! The awesome wonder of it! If God

can do *that* with a life like *hers,* what could he do with a life like mine, or yours? Oh! Let him touch you and teach you to be a blessing for him!

The world is waiting for a woman like you!

Section II
The Joyful Song of Loving

There is no proper preparation in the world for being a wife. From the moment you promise to love, honor, and join yourself to him, life is a process of adjustments. You and your husband are no longer two people, you are one; and your life together will be filled with joy and occasional sorrow. Here is a look at romance without the moonlight and roses. This is the broad daylight of love!

Several years ago I read the delightful little book *The Adventures of Being a Wife* by Mrs. Norman Vincent Peale. It was wonderfully entertaining, filled with the people she had met, the presidents with whom she had mingled, her travels, and the truths she had learned along the way! But after all, Mrs. Peale is married to Norman Vincent Peale. I maintain that her wifely "adventures" may be a bit different from mine! (I am not suggesting that Dr. Peale is perfect! There must be some dirty socks in his closet *somewhere*.) But he is, nevertheless, Dr. Peale, and as such he is possessed of fame, fortune, and several books full of positive thinking! Being his wife *would* be wonderful! But what about being a wife *period*? Wonderful! Still wonderful!

Never mind that most of us are ordinary mortals, in ordinary marriages. We have not been left with less! God's marvelous way is to give us *all* the joyful noise of loving, thus making *all* our lives captivating and vital. So there! Can love ever be called a "commonplace" experience? Not when it's *my* love, it can't! *My* love was made in heaven!

God does that for his own. He guides his children in their choices; he guards them; and he gives them wisdom to know his will. "All things work together for good to them that love God, to them who are called according to his purpose" (Rom.

8:28). And when two people love each other and the Lord, they are going to work together for good! That is how marriages are made in heaven!

And then, so that we won't undo what he has done for us, God has given us some guidelines for loving, his way. Not as the world would love, not as *we* would love, but as he loves, that's how we learn to love if we are his! God's love lasts and lasts and lasts. So should our love. This is a concept the world cannot understand—that one man and one woman would stay together, in love, lastingly. But this is how marriage was meant to be, his way! Some of the time we manage to do it his way. But some of the time . . .

Well, that is what this part of the book is about, the joyful song of loving. I've learned a lot in thirty years, but not nearly as much as I'm going to know thirty years from now! For it's constant, learning to live with the man you love. Continual. The days are filled with moments of emotion, feeling, moods, and the nights with wonder. The process never ends, and therein is the promise!

In a book about India, these delicate lines were written about a young man and a young woman who came together in an arranged marriage: "These two learned to be lovers like the waves that wash upon the shore, sometimes quiet and sometimes crashing. Beyond the shore there was always the horizon, blending earth and heaven, a line everlasting!"

Ah! How beautiful is being a wife! Being a wife is, what is the word I want? Oh, thank you, Mrs. Peale, being a wife is an ADVENTURE! Embark upon it! Embrace it! It's yours!

5
From Morning Until Night

My mother had a theory, "Get up with him in the morning, and go to bed with him at night, and everything else in between will work itself out!" That statement is not oversimplified. It is, in a nutshell, the secret of success in a marriage.

Oh, I don't mean to say that you don't need a lot of other things, other thoughts, prayers, patience, faith, and fortitude. Surely you do. But if you care about him, not just love him, not just like him, not just want him, if you CARE about him more than you CARE for yourself (and I believe that's what the Bible commands us wives to do), then you will "get up with him in the morning and go to bed with him at night," regardless of how you feel, physically, emotionally, mentally, at the moment! In other words, you will be *with* him, and when that is the case then everything else can be conquered.

Of course, he is supposed to be the same support to you! He is supposed to love you as he loves himself (Eph. 5:33). And sometimes he will. But sometimes he won't. He will be human. He will have his moody days, his down days, his temper tantrums, and his unreasonable outrages. (So will you, for that matter, but let's move on for the moment.)

The important thing is that you be *with* him without reservations! The Scripture doesn't say, "If he's in a good mood, be a wife to him," "If you've got the time and the temperament for it, be a wife to him," "If all is well and the day has gone right, and there's money in the bank, be a wife to him"! The Scripture says, "Woman [was created] for the man" (1 Cor. 11:9), and I have to believe it if the Bible says it.

And so, you will get up with him in the morning! Of course, there are exceptional cases. Some men do not eat breakfast, ever. Some men prefer the early solitude. Some men want a meal at the club after the 7 AM workout in the gym. But these men are few and far between. Most men want breakfast. Most men are rushed, already mentally running, long before they get to the office. Often they are tense about a meeting, worried about a co-worker, wondering how the day will go, and if they are able to take on the task. They need help—if not the physical help of getting the eggs and bacon (though that *is* a time-saver for them)—then the psychological help of someone to say, "You look great! You smell terrific! I'm looking forward to seeing you tonight! Have a good day! Darling, here's your lunch!"

You may not look glamorous. (Indeed, if you know anybody who *does* at breakfast, call me. I want to come over.) You may not even be able to converse in more than monosyllables. And there will be mornings when you will be such a mess, spill the milk, burn the toast black, make the mistake of asking him what he's going to wear to next week's date with the dinner club. On those days it certainly would have been better if you had stayed in bed. But the habit, the constant, continual habit of caring enough about him to be *with* him in the morning, will be a reassuring signal to you both through the years. It will say to you both: "Some things never change. We may be rich or poor or sick or well or old or young or sad or glad, but we are *together* at breakfast, for better or for worse!" Believe me. It is such a simple thing, but it is also such a comfort.

And then, from breakfast to bed! I like double beds! Great big, bouncy double beds! And lots of pretty, soft sheets and pillows for plopping, warm, woolly blankets, and downy comforters. Your bed should be the one single most thought-out, expensive, expressive thing in your house. Here you rest. Here you retreat when you are tired, weary, and worn. Here you relax, lying late in bed to watch the snow fall, fresh, white, bright, being glad you can't go to work or to school or to the civic center. Here, in bed, new life begins, in each others arms, blessed, beautiful. And here you love.

Certainly, there is more to love than sex! But there is no better way to give love or to receive it, and there is no surer sign that your lives and your love are on stable, steady ground than good sex! Sex is not to be underestimated because God did not underestimate it. He did not create for Adam a friend. He created for Adam a wife, a woman, a sexual partner. Thank goodness for sex in marriage, for without it our marriages would be just different levels of friendship shared. There is nothing wrong with friendship or sharing between husbands and wives. But that alone does not make a marriage.

I have friends, both men and women, whom I love. I have friends with whom I can go to lunch, tell secrets, travel. I have friends I can pray with and for, friends I can call about a problem, friends I can live with. I have friends with whom I can be a pleasant companion. And I can do all of these things with my husband!

The marvelous addition that makes it a marriage is sex! *That* I share only with him! And he with me! It is what makes us special, set apart, one, a "couple." It is the "must" in marriage. Sex is the one thing that should not be used as a reward or a punishment or a tool to manage or manipulate your partner. There should be no argument about sex from either the husband or the wife. You just do not say no to your husband. You just do not. Never. Ever.

In the first place, why would you want to?! Here is the man you love, and he is hungry. If he wanted a meal you would see to it that he had what he wanted, when he wanted it, whether you had a headache or not. If he needed medicine, you would call a doctor, no delays or lagging regardless of his likability at the moment. But what he wants, what he needs, is to make love! But, you say, he was cross with me this morning! He has been a bear since that business deal went sour. It was not *my* fault it fell through, and yet *I* have felt the fury of his frustration. I am terribly tired, and he hasn't even asked me about my day or answered me when I asked him about his. He hasn't touched me or been tender to me, and now he wants to play "Me Tarzan, You Jane!"

Well, you can complain all you please. You can declare to the world that he is unfair and unfriendly. You can maintain that he should notice you and be nice to you, and you will be absolutely correct! But you will not be right! The RULES say, Love "seeketh not her own" way, is not proud, is "not puffed up," "endureth" long and lastingly! The RULES say, Love "beareth all things, believeth all things," never fails! The fact is, I'm afraid, according to the RULES of love, you have no rights. What you *have* is a husband, and he is hungry. He wants to make love to you. If he is a Christian man and has made a commitment to you, making love is something he cannot buy, beg, borrow, or steal. He can receive it only from you. He can be satisfied only with you. He can make love only to you! Don't you feel honored? Don't you feel proud and necessary and needed? You should, for this is the natural response that God placed in you!

Here is the beauty of the blessing. When you approach love with the attitude that you have no rights, suddenly *you have everything*. Oh, I don't mean to say that there will be no more terrible times or no more valleys in between the mountaintops. It's just that there is no problem, no peak, no mountain that is insurmountable in the face of your husband's happiness in you! You will have not only his love and loyalty (which some Christian men continue to give even without the benefit of the marriage bed) but also you will have *him*, in ways that will make you marvel. And he will return to you, a thousand thoughtful times, the gift that you have given him, yourself!

There is no need for you to pretend a passion you do not feel. Women and men are different, as any basic biology class can tell you. Contrary to what Hollywood would have us believe, women are not always as ready to make love as men. There will be times, of course, when your emotions will match his in the most extraordinary manner, when "bells ring and birds sing," and with your love you could light the night sky. But more often than not you will be warm and willing simply because he wants you. You will have an emotional experience of giving, sharing, and caring as only you can care for him. And you will be glad, for now *you have everything*!

If in the end, you do *not* have everything, you will still have the peace of heart and mind and soul that you had done it "God's way" and not "my way." That, after all, is what really matters most, is it not? To do it God's way! To die to self and to serve: my man, my marriage, my calling, and my career— whatever, wherever he has led. It is the only way, God's way!

I am not writing, naturally, to couples who have problems and pains that are unique or unusual, problems that need to be tackled by a psychologist or a sociologist or a dedicated doctor. I am writing to the middle America Christian couple, to a man and a woman who are committed to Christ and to each other, and who want to stay married (and to be "happy in spite of it," as one of my special friends puts it!)

Not only will you be warm and willing when he wants you, but there will be times—because you love him and want his happiness and health—when you will seduce him. Seriously.

Our men have a way of becoming overweight and/or overworked, at least some of their lives, and that combination can be deadly to sex. Either condition is a *problem,* but together they can be a PROBLEM! After you have discovered the diet that he needs and after you have discussed his workhorse habits with him, there is little else you can do in *those* areas. But you *can* see to it that his sex life doesn't suffer. He needs you whether he knows it or not, and you must be the first to tell him. Gently. Always gently.

If he were working late at his desk and had not stopped for dinner, you would fix him a tray of tempting food and take it to him, with the gentle reminder that he must eat if he wants to be well. And if he hasn't stopped lately for the love of his life, you must take it to him!

I am not advocating any girlish games or naughty negligees on fifty-year-old women. Most intelligent men and women are long past such surface things. What I am suggesting is a gentle closeness, a touching, a tenderness, an exchange of words that tells him, "I want you to be happy and healthy because I love you so. Your body needs mine. Your spirit needs mine. And we must be together." Certainly, you will be careful not to approach this plan when he is too tired or too anxious or totally unprepared. You do not wish to demand, but to give. You may speak of the subject several times, in several ways, over several days. You may need to arrange the time and the atmosphere. You may even need to ask him to *help* you to arrange it all.

There is absolutely nothing wrong with arranged sex. We arrange everything else in our lives that is important: our education, our finances, our social engagements, our dentist and doctor appointments, even our times of prayer and Bible reading. How often have you *not* felt like praying? How often have you *not* felt like reading your Bible? But because you have arranged a time of the day or the week in which you always do this, you continue to return to that time and are blessed by it! Where would we be without arranged times and places to meet, to eat, to work, to worship? Why on earth should sex be any different? Certainly, it would be wonderful if life ran well without our making lists of things to do and places to be and people to see. But that is not the case. Sometimes praying is spontaneous, and sometimes it is not. A spontaneous time of seeing friends or writing or reading or wandering through musty museums can be wonderful. But often only a well-organized, well-ordered, *planned* day is wonderful. Both are beautiful.

And so, sometimes sex is spontaneous. Indeed, since it is such a tremendous human drive, sex is *usually* spontaneous. But sometimes, for any number of reasons, it isn't. Husbands carry the weight of the world on their shoulders. Love wears thin when there is more work and worry than they can carry. But a man's body was made in such a way as to need the release of tensions, both psychological and physical, in that special love relationship with his wife. There are times when a caring, sharing wife will be the one to encourage this relationship. Not only does she do this for him but also for herself. Therefore, whenever there is the need, she will be the one to make him aware once more of the woman in his home!

You see, you are to love him more than you love yourself. His needs are more important to you than your own. I am not saying that we women always manage to live like we believe this. We are mortals, and often we are mortally selfish. We'd rather have a new car than a bank balance or a walk in the woods than doing dishes or *Gone With the Wind* than Monday night football. Often, I fear, we want our needs "first and foremost," in lots of little ways. But we must make certain that in the *big* ways we love and love and love again like the Lord says we should.

6
To Cherish or to Choke

We had been telling each other secrets since we were in our teens. Now our children played nearby. I remember we were sitting at the round redwood table behind my house. The honeysuckle was heavy, fresh, and fragrant. It was fall, and the small yellow leaves of the cedar oak fell around us with each bit of breeze and into the pool, floating there like pale embroidery on blue satin. And suddenly I saw the tears on her face. "Oh, Joy," she whispered, "I'm married to a wonderful man, but . . . "

Two hours later she went home to that wonderful man, loving him, liking him, but so burdened by the differences that divided them.

Again, I remember a Sunday morning. This time I was sitting in the soft sunlight that streamed through the glorious stained-glass windows of our sanctuary. A few people lingered at the front, but most had left. The girl beside me was a bride of mere months, but on her face also were tears. She seemed to me to be the same little girl I had led in Girls Auxiliary. "Oh, Mrs. Davis! I'm married to a wonderful man, but . . . "

In a few moments she went out to meet that wonderful young man with whom she had made a strong and stable marriage, but she was still so saddened by the misunderstanding that had caused her to cry.

Once I considered writing a magazine series called, "I'm Married to a Wonderful Man, But!" I have heard that same sentence said so many times through the years by so many brides, both old and young! It's as if the words were handed from generation to generation, a "password" for a sorority of sisters. What has actually happened, of course, is that the world is full of women who are married to wonderful men, but the human race is "fraught with frailties." Women have them. Men have them. And nowhere are we more "frail" than in marriage!

I am fond of my flamboyant friend who gesticulates a lot as she rants and raves. One day she was giving me a list of grievances against her man that was a mile long. She paused briefly for breath, and I reminded her lightly, "Remember! You promised to *cherish* him!"

"*Cherish* him?" she screamed. "I am going to *choke* him as soon as I see him!"

Well, don't we all feel that way sometimes! No matter how much we want, need, love, adore, and dote on our husbands, there are times that are simply too terrible to cherish! To choke would definitely be a better verb.

Why in the world is that? People are not perfect. People in love are especially not perfect. And the problem is compounded because people in love usually live in the same house! Living in the same house with someone of the opposite sex is an arrangement with ready-made pitfalls, like lost privacy and takenover territory and ever-present compromise! How can we possibly avoid aggravation, sometimes *serious* aggravation?! Certainly, we do not eliminate it from our lives. Indeed, we add to it another ingredient, *acceptance*.

Love is a lot of things, and one of them is acceptance. Acceptance is a large part of the Christian life, as we accept God's assignments, as we accept sickness and sorrow and hurt in an imperfect world, as we accept the happiness that we have. But nowhere is acceptance more needed and necessary than in one's love life. Here it is not only important but it is also imperative!

We *say*, perhaps, that we accept the men we love, with all their warts and that we wouldn't want them any other way! But sometimes we say this outwardly, while inwardly we want them to become the men we have imagined! (I am not speaking, naturally, of spiritual matters. Certainly, if our loved ones are not saved then we must be bent on bringing them to the Lord.) I am writing to Christians, and acceptance is an area in which Christians have a difficult time. The non-Christian would have an "easy out." The non-Christian would say, "Why learn to accept when to leave or to live and let live is so much easier?" The Christian couple, meanwhile, in order to develop that vital relationship that is so valuable, must learn the art of acceptance! Does it sound simple? It isn't!

There may be hundreds of things you love about your man, and only one you don't love. But as the years go on, and on, and on, that one thing may become the thorn that tears your heart apart *unless* you have learned acceptance! Now, early in marriage the young wife often learns to accept dirty shirts dropped in unlikely places, disorganized desks and work benches, and the weekly golf game. (Young husbands will, meanwhile, be learning to accept a lot also, like rollers and cold cream and wives who are late.) But these are relatively simple side effects from living with a person of the opposite sex. What takes all the soul's sensibilities is learning to accept the *person* within that man's body or that woman's body. It is an accomplishment which comes only with years of trial and error, and it is continuous.

I have a friend who has been close to me for thirty years. She is a wonderful woman in many ways—deep, dedicated, and multitalented. She has raised a houseful of children, made her husband a happy man, and carried on a career. She is a master student of the Bible and is an intuitive teacher of the Word. If anybody could manage acceptance easily, you would think she could, yet she tells me that it has been an almost elusive quest through the years. Hers is a problem repeated in hundreds of homes: her husband works sixteen hours a day. He has *always* worked sixteen hours a day. It is because he absolutely loves his work. He long ago reached the peak of his profession. He long ago made enough money to provide for his family forever. It is simply that he enjoys his work. He works when everyone else goes home, goes on vacation, or goes away for the weekend. He is not driven by any deep, dark personality traits. He is not angry at the world or out to prove himself as a person. He just likes to do what he does.

But this has left my friend alone for more days and nights than she cares to count. She is a strong person, and we're all glad because she has had to do a lot of things alone like mow the yard, clean the pool, take the kids to their doctors and dentists and play practices, not to mention trips to emergency rooms for broken legs and lacerated heads. She has had to get them off in the morning and tuck them in at night, alone, because her husband left before they got up and returned after they were in bed. Whether it was the carpet, the canary, or the refrigerator that needed fixing, *she* decided whom to call, when, and where. Except for a two-week summer trip and Sunday mornings, the family was without a father.

For years, my friend moaned and groaned about this. She cried. She prayed. She implored her husband for help in solving the situation. She was always careful to cover for him, and the children loved him for the quality of their time with him if not for the quantity, but my friend grew very, very weary. Besides, she was lonely. As a young wife she would try to wait up for him at night, hoping to have some time with him. She would finally fall asleep on the couch. He would tiptoe past her (at midnight or whenever) careful not to awaken her. The next morning when she woke up on the couch and found him sleeping in their bed, she was furious. Understandably so. It wasn't that she didn't love him. It wasn't that she wanted to leave him. There were, in fact, hundreds of ways in which he was a man to be admired and respected. She was proud and pleased to be his wife. But she was lonely and tired too! And so she cried and prayed that he would change, that eventually they would have a regulated life, that eventually he would become the man in her imagination!

Then one day it dawned on her that he was not going to change! He was not ever going to become regulated. His life would never be nine to five. The solution was so simple. She would learn to accept him as he was.

My friend learned almost immediately that this took a lot of analyzing. First, from the personal standpoint, she had to realize that her husband's habits had nothing to do with how he felt about her. He loved her and would have given her whatever she wanted, if he could have understood what she wanted. But his habits were so much a part of him and he was so placid in his pattern that her words were a foreign language to him. Therefore, realizing that his habits had nothing to do with her personally, my friend's approach to the acceptance of the situation could be completely clinical.

Second, from the practical standpoint, she realized that she had been given by God an added measure of strength, physically and mentally. She was *able* to mow the yard, clean the pool, and race to the emergency room. Therefore, God must have prepared her for this personal situation. She should be glad that he had known what she would need!

Third, she knew that her demands for her husband to be different were detrimental to peace of mind, his *and* hers. There remained, then, only the need to know how to be quiet. If she were going to accept, truly, then she knew she must not mention it again!

Once she was quiet, things began to be better! Oh, I don't mean that her husband stopped working sixteen hours a day. That has not changed because *he* has not changed. But now he is free to be the person that he is, naturally. He is free to love his wife, his work, his children, and his church in the way that was destined by his distinct individuality. It may not be the way his wife once imagined, but it is the only way *he* can imagine, and now she accepts it. The relief has been limitless! He is free of trying to change. She is free of trying to make him change. Everybody has so much more energy!

The prayer of serenity became hers in a personal, permanent way, "Lord, grant me the courage to change what I can change, to accept what I cannot change, and the grace to know the difference!"

There is one more step we must take if we want to master this marvelous acceptance that can free so many from so much frustration. It is this: not only must we learn to accept, but also we must learn to accept *joyfully*! If I never, ever make it in any other area of my Christian life, I want to learn to accept joyfully! There must be no overtones of the "martyr." The acceptance of your loved one is a gift, and it must be given gloriously in order to be fully effective for both of you!

My own quest for joyful acceptance has been, as my friend said, "almost elusive." But I believe I may make it. *My situation is simply that my husband does not talk much.* (How could he? *I'm* always talking.) But notwithstanding marriage to me, he does not naturally verbalize a lot. It is not his nature to share the mental process by which he makes his decisions, formulates his ideas, or proceeds with his work. He does not naturally discuss his attitudes about life or his positions on any subject. He *states* his views or his reasons. He does not *discuss* them. It takes a lot less time to state than to discuss, believe me. And for a long time, to me, this left a lot to be desired. I wanted to discuss. I love to ask questions. He, however, does not like the QUIZZ.

When I make a statement I am likely to say the same thing in three different ways. When I ask a question I am likely to ask three different questions that require one and the same answer. To him, this is wasted effort and not worth bothering about. He was frustrated at having to come up with answers. I was frustrated at not getting all the information. I want the background, the beginning, the middle of the story, not just the ending. When I tell a tale, whether it be my adventures at the supermarket or how I spent my summer vacation, I tell it from beginning to end. Likewise for how I ran the red light, forgot my door keys, or failed to stub an outstanding check—beginning to end. How many times, I can't tell you, he has interrupted my tale with, "The bottom line, Joy! The bottom line!" But simple, declarative statements seem to be beyond me.

Also, I didn't just *want* to know the whole story, I was *used* to knowing everything about the man in my life. When I was little, my father was a talkative man. He would talk for hours to my mother or me—whether we were listening or not. Whatever was on his mind—a bother, a problem, or simply a new program for his people—he talked about it from morning until night. We always knew where he was in his thinking. He said so. Therefore it was doubly hard for me not to know everything my husband was thinking. I wondered why he did this or that, not that I doubted his decision. I was just curious. Not that I didn't trust his timing or his method or even his "madness," as the saying goes, I just wanted to know more!

Then one day it dawned on me. I was never going to know more. He was never going to detail for me his thoughts. I would just have to wonder. I would accept. So simple, so simple it has taken me thirty years.

I've always been aware that there are very real and valid reasons why my husband does not discuss his work with me. It is partly because he would rather shield me than share it with me, and it is partly because he would rather not "rehash" it after hours. He would rather leave it at work. But this worried me, especially when I could see *he* was worried or weary or depressed. He was obviously in some problem-solving situation. Perhaps there were conflicts or confusions with the people at the office; and if I only knew, I thought, I would know what to say or do or how to help. At least I would like to *listen* to him. But it was not to be so.

Finally, as I began to accept, I also began to see what a real relief it was to me *not* to know all the things he wasn't saying. So what if there is a problem at the plant or with the people on the project? So what if the parts are held up at the airport? Does this really matter to me? What *matters* to me is his peace of mind. If to let him alone is the answer *he* needs, then that is all the answer *I* need. And when he's cross, do I really care? I know (if I think about it for sixty seconds) that it is not pointed at me personally. It isn't that he is cross with me but with himself, his boss, his secretary, or the mechanic on the line. Surely I can see this and let it alone. When you think about it, if your husband handles problems like mine does, do you really want to know all the things that are wrong at work? Mercy, no. Thank heaven for a man who doesn't bother you with it. Do you really want to know all he went through to arrive at the right decision? Goodness, no. Thank heaven for a man who doesn't bore you with it. The end result is all that matters, his peace of mind.

So, the decision is made. If your husband solves his problems without discussing them in detail with you, let him alone. Everything else is secondary. Although you once imagined that the man in your life would talk to you, ask you for advice, speak to you for inspiration, *he* did not imagine that he would. *He* imagined that he would work it all out for himself. Once you accept this, look at the relief! You are free to use your energies elsewhere. And *he* is free of the frustration of trying to tell you everything when he would rather rest his mind of the matter!

There are many things in life that we can change—acquired habits that threaten our health or learned temperaments (anxious or angry) that threaten our happiness. But we cannot change the inborn traits of our personalities any more than we can change the color of our eyes. We are born to be fast or slow or talkative. Our body clocks go off at different times. Therefore, once you realize that your mate *cannot* do whatever it is you want (because he was not born to do it), then you will be well on your way to a clinical acceptance of the situation. Be thankful for him as he is. He is different from you! How interesting! What cause for rejoicing! Now, you see?! You are learning the secret of joyful acceptance!

Acceptance is so much more than a grim determination to grit your teeth and bear it. It is learning to be *happy* that your man is the man he is. After all, his individuality, like yours, is divinely inspired. Accepting him does not mean you must change. He has not changed. You need not change. Your traits are as much a truth as his. You accept that person within his body because you love him and want to live with him in happiness and peace!

The marriage vows did not say, "I will love you if you are like the man I imagined." The marriage vows say, "I will love you!"

So, not only do we accept each other's inborn body traits, chemistry, and characteristics but we also accept each other's faults. Once more it is mandatory that we see these solely for what they are, faults, not actions or reactions that have anything to do with us personally. Your approach to the acceptance of this situation also must be clinical, not personal, if it is to be successful.

As a wife, strive to understand *why* he is the way he is, *what* has caused the temper, the mood, the melancholy, *how* you can help. More often than not, there were facts in his life, forces, long before he loved you that laid the foundation for these faults. You may not ever be able to erase the effect of these forces on his life, but you can see them for what they are, facts, and know that they have nothing to do with you or his deep-down love for you. *You* may be the one to feel these faults that are born of his fears or frustrations because if his *boss* felt them your man might be fired! He knows it, and you know it. So try to see it from his side, always, since that is where you should be, on his side!

I *know* you would rather be a good "sounding board" than a "scapegoat," but sometimes his actions and reactions are going to make you miserable. Face it, for it is a fact! But try, try, try to "share his shoes," as the old English proverb puts it. Soon you will sympathize. He needs your sympathy! So sympathize, silently!

Perhaps the most precious insight to acceptance was given to me by an older woman, someone who had lived for a long time with one man. Her husband was a doctor, a "beloved physician" in the city.

"He never said I'M SORRY!" she sighed, then added with a fanciful smile on her face, "Well, *almost* never!"

Her composure as a person was beautiful to see, the result of the patience that had become a part of her. She was calm, therefore, those around her were calm. I leaned back, relaxed, and listened.

She told me of a time, after she and he had been married for twenty years, when he was terribly tired and fell into a deep depression. Several things contributed to the depression—the loss of his father, the failing mobility of his mother, their son's separation from his wife. Being depleted, physically and mentally, he could not come to terms with it all and became increasingly distressed. He worked at the hospital as well as ever, but at home he was another man, morose, moody. He became surly, accusing her of causing his unhappiness. He could not bear to blame himself. Of course, he could deal with his father's sudden death, his mother's sickness, and his son's separation. What was *wrong* in his life was his *wife*! It was so hurtful, so sad, to hear him say those things to her. She was brokenhearted.

At the same time she realized that he was not himself. She knew what had happened to him, and she knew that the pain of the experience had left him confused and afraid. Even as she prayed for him and for herself, weeping out her own despair and pain, she could honestly plead, "Father, forgive him, for he knows not what he does. Be gentle with him, God! He is wounded. He will be well again."

And he was well again. He was a believer, and slowly, surely, the light returned to his life. He was once more the man she married, thoughtful, wise, and witty. But he never said, "I'm sorry." He never did. The months passed, and she remembered the pain. She was thankful each day that her thoughtful husband was once more himself, that their marriage was once more secure and caring. But he never said, "I'm sorry." He never held her to him and said, "I know what a terrible time it was for you last summer. I know how I hurt you. I am grateful to God that you understood and stayed and prayed, and I love you for it. I am so sorry." He never did that. After many months, it began to be a source of real sadness for the wife. She would pray and read the Word and cry out, "Lord, doesn't he *know* how he crushed me? Doesn't he *know*?"

Then one day it dawned on her. He did *not* know, and it was by the mercy of the Lord that he did not know! Suddenly she remembered all those mornings when she would go into the garden and weep and pray, "Father, forgive him! God, be gentle with him. He is a good man, and he deserves a good wife. He is afraid and confused. He has been wounded, but he will be well again. Let him live again, this good man! Return him to me!"

And God had done so! She knew now that she must not only accept her husband but also her answered prayer for him. She saw now that if her husband truly *knew* how he had hurt her that he could not begin to bear it. Here was a man who loved her. To truly *know* what he had done to her would leave him desperate, despairing of ever gaining her love again. With his mind, he remembered the terrible time, of course, and was grateful to God that it was over for both of them. But with his heart he never knew the depth of the pain he had caused his partner. And it was by the mercy of the Lord that he did not!

Now she could rejoice! Her husband had not said, "I'm

sorry." But now she could accept, joyfully, seeing that God had indeed been gentle with her good man, sparing him knowledge that would have overwhelmed him.

Oh, *that* is acceptance! Celestial acceptance!

And finally, you need to go another mile! The first mile is learning to live with the man you love in sweet acceptance. It is an accomplishment of which you can be proud. Although you can never know another person completely, you now know enough about your man to help keep the "peaceable kingdom" content, and if not always content, at least intact! See, then, the second mile! Pass this understanding, this sweet acceptance, on to the little people in that "kingdom"!

A child knows only that the temperament and mood are not loving at the moment. He cannot separate the moment from forever. He feels he is at fault. *You* know he isn't. You must make sure *he* knows he isn't.

When your husband, who is wonderful, is sometimes short with himself and everyone else, including the children of the household, *explain* him to them. *Explain* him to them so that you are all on the *same* side, though possibly with differing opinions. You have learned acceptance. You have learned to see the situation with love. Show it to the children that way. Tuck them in and tell them, "Dad grew up without much money. He is simply a saving person. He was cross when he felt we wanted something he could not afford," or, "Dad did not learn to hug as a little boy. We must love him lots and lots to make up. He may never be as 'huggy' as we would want, but that does not mean he does not love us. He does, dearly," or, "Today when Dad fussed and fumed about everything and nothing at all, he was not mad at you, or us, but himself. He's had a bad day," or, "I'm sorry Dad missed your music recital on Tuesday and your game on Thursday, but we must let him know we are thankful he takes care of us in many other ways!" *Explain* him to them, sincerely, justly, joyfully. Teach them the acceptance you have learned!

Surely, I am not talking about serious situations, such as mental or physical abuse. I am talking about ordinary people, in ordinary love relationships. I am talking about leading children to understand the temperament of the people they love. And when you have done this, you have then managed several things, all of them marvelous. You have saved the children's security. You have retained their relationship with their father. You have prepared them to be compassionate people for life. And you have given your husband your greatest service since you said "I do"!

I have seen this "service" in several families through the years, and it is always a wonder to watch. I have known wonderful women married to wonderful men who were dynamic, prosperous, prominent, and cross. I have known kind women married to kind men who were loyal, brave, brilliant, and distant. These are faults, and they are hard to live with, much less love. How hurt and humiliated and lost for life some children would be if parents thoughtlessly left them alone to sort out adult temperaments and moods. (The fact that adult temperaments and moods are more often than not childish is beside the point here.) Nevertheless, a little love and a lot of understanding at the right time and place can smooth the wrinkles away from an otherwise rumpled relationship!

To cherish: It's an easier verb to conjugate!

7
Having, but Mostly Holding

Help me! I need you to help me! You would think that when someone cried that to a loved one help would be forthcoming. Alas! *Help* is a word that means different things to different people. The greatest divergence in definition seems to fall between men and women! *Help* to most women means "talk to me." *Help* to most men, however, means "leave me alone." The problem then, lies in helping those men for whom *help* means "leave me alone" to at least at times translate *help* as "talk."

Most men's minds are programmed to be problem-solving mechanisms. They see situations as clear-cut question and answer. So when such a man sees his wife sitting in the middle of the bed crying, he wants to know why. Is it a problem with the plumbing, the car, the cat, the kids? Then call the repair people or the vet or the teacher, but beyond that, what on earth can *he* do about it? If your husband is like this, he could hold you. Sometimes he may do that. Sometimes he may not.

Worse yet than crying when you have a problem is when you are sitting in the middle of the bed crying and you don't know why. You can't tell your husband or you don't tell him or you won't tell him or all three. Then he may *really* throw up his hands. What he should do, of course, is hold you some more. He should sit down beside you and put his arms around you and tell you he knows you are blue, beside yourself, and here is his handkerchief! What he will do is to throw up his hands.

Part of the reason for this reaction is because questions without answers "do not compute" in many men's minds. But part of the reason (and I've only recently learned this) may be that they find their wives' tears frightening. You see, most men tend to think of their women as emotionally strong, just as most women tend to think of their men as physically strong. We think this because it is usually true. Most men *are* stronger physically than most women. And most women *are* stronger emotionally than most men. Men build houses. Women make houses into homes. (We can overlap roles and often do for lots of reasons, most of them good, but that does not change the physical, mental, and emotional traits that are typically identified as masculine and feminine.)

Therefore, when a man sees his woman crying, weeping over Lord knows what, he may be more than frustrated. He may be frightened. This is not the emotionally strong, stable woman he knows. This is not the mother who can cope with crisis, as he has seen her do; the wife who stands with him through thick and thin, as he has seen her do; the career woman who has just gotten a raise; the Christian woman who is admired by many as a model to emulate. No, this weeping woman is someone he does not know! Subconsciously, or even consciously, he may even wish she were not weak at this moment. Therefore, the man who feels *frustration* at not knowing why the tears flow and *fear* that they do indeed flow often does not do the one thing that might take care of those tears. He does not comfort his wife.

Sometimes this does not matter. Many women can weep by themselves and feel better afterward. But for other women it does matter whether they receive comfort from their husbands. When time and time again they receive no comfort, soon these women feel lost and alone, isolated from their husbands.

One woman told me, "The books about human sexuality all tell me that women have as many sexual fantasies as men! Well, I have a fantasy, all right, but it has nothing to do with sex. Over and over again I see myself sitting alone, perhaps by a window with rain pouring down outside, crying as if my heart would break. Suddenly there are arms around me, holding me close, gentle, just holding me. I never know who's arms they are. There is never a face in my fantasy. I just know it is not my husband!"

Another woman was more candid. "I'd never leave my husband for a sexual affair with another man," she told me, "but if I ever met a man who knew how to hold me when I hurt, now there would be *some* temptation!"

Perhaps the most poignant statement of all came from a young woman, small-boned and beautiful, her face almost fragile, with pale skin, blue eyes, blond hair. There was not a soul in the house that summer's day except the two of us, yet she lowered her voice as if it were too sad to say aloud, "When I cry," she whispered, "nobody comes!" Such loneliness is not necessary.

The man who could learn the fine art of attentiveness at a time like this would be rewarded with a wife who would bloom and blossom and become more beautiful each time he touched her!

The coin, of course, has two sides. The woman who knows how to help her husband, whether by leaving him alone or listening to him, will endear herself to her husband.

Maybe you just need to be close enough to care for your husband's physical needs while he is working out a problem. Your husband may work out the matter almost mathematically. If so, give him the time to himself that he needs. Most men are deliberate. Some men do not need to talk through the stages of decisions the way some women do. One day they have a problem, and the next day, or the next month or the next year, it is solved.

The same coin, with the same two sides, may apply when the two of you have grievances. When you have had an argument, *you* may want to make up immediately. *He* may want to wait awhile. If this is the situation in your home, give him some silence, some solitude, some time. Then, when he wants to talk, let him talk without interruption. (There are many ways of doing this. Masking tape across the mouth is a last resort, of course, but should, nevertheless, be left on the list.)

So you want to talk, and he wants to be left alone. Each of you can try to accommodate the other, but it wouldn't be all bad to try to reverse roles either! He can learn to find a real relief in your loving listening if he would share with you his thoughts, his worries, his weaknesses, instead of shutting you out until he has it all resolved himself. How much easier it would be for him through the nights and days of his life if he would let you love him, talk to him, even offer him your words of wisdom.

Also, when you need his shoulder to cry on, he should realize that, it would be over so much sooner if he could share with you that shoulder, if he could remember that although you are capable of calling the plumber, the vet, or the teacher, and will do so soon, sometimes you need to cry, preferably with him beside you!

Hold each other. It may not make sense, but it sure makes a solid marriage!

You will notice that I have never said, "Husbands should give their wives more time." Women don't need *time,* as such. They need *tenderness.* There is a difference. When a woman says, "You don't pay enough attention to me," she means exactly what she says, attention = tenderness. But a man may interpret attention as *time.* He will counter with, "What in the world do you want me to do? Give up my job so I can be with you every minute of every day? Give up my golf, my hunting, my fishing? There's just so much time in every day, you know!" But she did not ask for time. (When asking for attention from her husband, a woman may ask for "time," meaning attention-translated-tenderness!)

Women do not need their men every minute of every day. Women are prepared by nature to "nest" on their own for long *periods* of time, actually, and to accomplish a great deal while doing it. Women, in fact, have been saying good-bye to their men for centuries—sending them off to crusades, wars, buffalo hunts, shrimp boats, diplomatic missions, and executive suites. Women are capable of being left alone and of managing alone all the mild and major crises that may develop while they are alone.

What women are *not* prepared by nature to endure is a lack of personal attention, or tenderness, from their men when they *are* at home. What women need, by nature, is the touching, the little looks that say, "I'm so glad you are with me, that you are mine, that you hear me, listen to me, love me. What would I ever do without you?" (Come to think of it, the "little looks" are wonderful, but the "little *words*" would be even more wonderful! Actually *hearing* those things now and then would be heaven!)

Men are marvelous at providing materially. They work eight to ten hours a day, then come home to roof the house, wax the car, mow the yard, fix the fence. They then fall into bed feeling they have been good husbands. And they HAVE been! But the tiny touch over the table at dinner, the loving look, the whispered words at the end of the day, "I love you! I'm too tired to say more, but as you sleep, sleep sweetly, because we are together!" Those are the things which turn a *good* husband into a *great* one!

You see, something has to be there besides sex. In the young days, with the babies, the bottles, and the 2:00 AM feedings, and the constant climb to the top of the professional peak, at least there was lots of sex. You were young and passionate and playful. And though sex doesn't take the *place* of tenderness, actually there should be an abundance of both, at least you were together intimately for a time each day. But life moves on to middle age and past, and the passion, while just as sweet, is not as persistent as once it was. *Then* you need the tenderness between you like never before! *Then* you need the touching, the little looks, the whispered words, as never, ever before!

First You Cry is a book by Betty Rollin, the respected newspaper woman, about her courageous battle with breast cancer. In the television adaptation of the book, there is a scene, before the trial of illness begins, between Mrs. Rollin and her husband (Mary Tyler Moore and Tony Perkins). They are sharing a companionable moment in bed before saying good night. He kisses her and smiles playfully, "Does that count? You always said bed kisses don't count!"

There is not a woman in the world who does not understand that statement. "Bed kisses" do count, of course. But the fact remains that "bed kisses," for both of you, are usually the preliminary to making love. This is mutual and marvelous, and you wouldn't want it any other way, but to a woman's heart, her emotional heart, the kisses that count have nothing to do with bed! The kisses that *count* come from your husband when you are suddenly sentimental over an old keepsake, and he sees it and kisses your tiny tears away; when you are suddenly so happy over an accomplishment, and he shares the moment and kisses you for making him happy too! And the kisses that count *double* are the ones that come for no reason at all: when he simply kisses you because you are there, when you pass him in the hall, when you are picking mint leaves off the lattice, when you are reading or rolling your hair, with your mind a million miles away! If men only knew! Most women would exchange luxuries for life for kisses like that!

Just remember! Helpmates are to have, but mostly to hold!

8
Football Fever

If we women are going to "forgive and forget" all the times we feel misunderstood, unnoticed, or neglected, then we must know more about *why* our men do not notice, or do not understand, some of the deepest desires of our hearts. Simply to say, "Men are men, and women are women," does not suffice day after day. We women know, of course, that our men are different from us physically and psychologically—but we know it mostly with our heads. We tend to forget it with our hearts, and it is then that we expect to get from them things they were not fashioned to give, like total attention at all times. We will *get* attention from our good husbands, of course. But total attention at all times is a far-fetched expectation!

Men have many levels on which they live. (Women do too, certainly, especially women who are as excited by their careers as they are by their love relationships.) But the levels of life for a woman are, more often than not, rather intricately connected. Her levels are more likely to overlap. The married woman is much more likely to consider her home and her husband as her "nucleus," with her career as an embellishment of an already complete picture.

But to most men, the picture is not complete without their work, and the levels in their lives tend to be seen as separate. A man can be deeply devoted to his love relationship on one level and on another level be equally committed to his career. On *that* level his profession is the most profound interest he has. On *that* level his business is not an embellishment. It is his life. It would have been his life if he had never met you or loved you or married you. Most men seem to have been prepared by nature to protect, provide, compete physically and mentally, and to relish the rivalry of other men, whether for play or for profit.

And where would we be if it were not so? Who would conquer the world? My modern psychology answers, "Amazons, that's who! Or Joan of Arc. Or Madam Curie! It isn't *nature* that has prepared men to provide and protect. It is *society* that has dictated these roles for them!"

Oh. I see. But was it society that created man first and gave him work, and then created woman second? Now wait a minute before you scream! I did *not* say woman was created to be secondary. I said woman was created second. But the fact remains that man was given work before he was given woman. And the fact remains that a man's work is usually vital to his survival. This is *sometimes* true for a woman, too, but it is almost *always* true for a man!

Certainly, men are often tired and tempted to walk away from the office or shop. Certainly, some men would prefer other professions. Surely, they often sing a sad song about the "corporate climb," recession, or the "rat race." But take a man's work away from him and he would wilt.

I am simply saying that most men have abilities and ambitions that have nothing whatever to do with us as wives. It is wonderful that we encourage them and are concerned, but whatever our husbands do professionally, they would probably have done just as well without us. Note that I said *professionally.* I did not say they would have done just as well without us *personally. Naturally* we are needed on the personal level. Naturally if a man wants to be a husband, a parent, or a partner-for-life in a love relationship, he needs a wife! But if he wants to be an engineer he needs a slide-rule. It is a separate level of his life.

Sometimes this is not easy for us women to accept. Many of us want to be important to every part of our husbands' lives, but we are not. And there is no need to feel ignored, neglected, or "left out." We need to know that there are separate levels in their lives, and that these levels are not "higher" or "lower" than the level of the love relationship, just "separate"!

Now I'm going to tell you about football! I don't know what it is with your man—golf, bowling, baseball, rod-and-reel, running—but if you can understand men's games, you can understand men! (You're not laughing are you? It's true, true, *true!*) And in Texas the name of the game is football!

In fact, even before I found myself in Texas, before TV, before Phyllis George and color-commentary, the men in my family loved football! I have vivid Mississippi memories of my father huddled over the radio, breathlessly quarterbacking Glenn Davis and Doc Blanchard in the Army-Navy game. I also have the memories of New Year's Eve, leaving Mississippi at 1 AM (*after* the Watch Night Service at the church) and driving to New Orleans in time for the Sugar Bowl on New Year's Day.

Then I married and moved to Dallas where football fever never cools. This is the land of the Cotton Bowl and the Cowboys, with a lot of Mustang Mania from Southern Methodist University and with the Baylor Bears only two hours away. This is a place where people plan their *lives* around football. You set dates for weddings, reunions, revivals, and coming-out parties with a football schedule in hand (that is, if you want people to *attend* whatever it is you're planning)!

I used to wonder why grown men played football, especially since it is a known fact that most professional football players are terribly intelligent. Most of them are college graduates, many have advanced degrees, some are Rhodes Scholars. Most of them are men who could succeed at anything on earth. Why, then, would they want to spend Sunday afternoon hitting and getting hit? Never mind the mental challenge of the game. If what they wanted was a mental challenge, they could find that in any executive suite! (And executive suites are safer, by far, than football fields.)

Only lately have I learned that most young males *enjoy* the combat, the bodily use of brute strength. This does not mean that their natures are brutal. Many of the biggest, roughest, toughest are gentle giants. It is simply that most young males enjoy the exercise of strength against strength. It is exhilarating to them. It is intensely interesting to them. Often it hurts, more than they ever imagined, although never enough to make them want to give up the game! (But tell me truthfully. Haven't you ever felt the same way about loving? Nothing in the world hurts as hard or as long as being in love, but never enough to make us want to "give up the game." And what about *having* babies? Now *that* hurts! But we keep on having them, hoping to have them, and planning to have them with great abandon, the pain of the experience notwithstanding!) Well, many men are that way about physical, mental, intellectual competition. They thrive on the thrill of it! This is usually a distinctive trait in men, even as nurturing is usually a distinctive trait in women. There are times when overlapping occurs. Men do, indeed, nurture their children, and women often work at careers or callings. But we must understand what is distinctive in the nature of our men, what they will do "naturally." Men are just naturally going to spend a lot of time "conquering the world" with or without us. Once we understand this, with our hearts as well as our heads, we will not demand from our men things they were not fashioned to give, like total attention at all times! Once you understand this, you can come to terms with it!

But back to football in Texas. (That is as good a place to "come to terms" as any.) For instance, many people in Texas act as if since the Pilgrims and the Indians shared their corn-on-the-cob one winter day in New England there has never been another Thanksgiving Day without football! And we all know it is purely impossible to have a formal Thanksgiving Day dinner on top of the TV. If your family cares this much about football, come to terms. Try having Thanksgiving dinner on Thanksgiving *eve* instead of Thanksgiving Day! Bake your turkey and all the trimmings on Wednesday! At twilight, light the candles. Your men are clean, dressed, handsome, and hungry when they come to the table. (It is, after all, the end of the day and they are famished. What better place to be, they think, than at your turkey table!) Everyone ohs and ahs over the beautiful bird, the creative napkin rings you made, the new recipe for asparagus-supreme. There is conversation. (Oh, you do *too* remember what that is: people talking to other people!) And then they dawdle over dessert, lavish with their compliments and praise. It is the kind of Thanksgiving that Good Housekeeping loves to look at!

Then, Thanksgiving Day dawns. The two TV sets flash in full color from one college stadium to another. There before your eyes is the football field, the excitement, the stampede of people, Phyllis George. Your men are in pajamas or blue-jeans. Who cares. The buffet is filled with lovely left-overs, platters of turkey and pumpkin pie, enough even for relatives, friends, and people you never saw who will drop in and out during the day. (And, if you enjoy football as much as your men, now you are free to watch play and replay!)

If not, you can sleep in. Nobody notices. Nobody needs you. They will have yesterday's candied yams for breakfast. When you do get up and greet the day, it's yours. My favorite thing to do on Thanksgiving Day is to address the Christmas cards. (It's the sort of simple assignment that can be done even under chaotic conditions. The dining room table is free for me and my cards since everyone else—friends, relatives, people I never saw—are eating on the buffet, the bed, the floor, whatever their vantage point for viewing the game!) During half-times you can watch the bands, while the men go outside to throw a football back and forth. Then during the second-half you can take a nap. (Get up in time to see the coach carried off the field. Everybody will think you have been there all the time.)

At the end of the day, the Christmas cards are stacked and stamped, ready to mail December 10. My memory of my picture-perfect Thanksgiving dinner is still special and warm and spicy. Most importantly, my men have not been hassled or prodded or pushed into suffering through a semblance of "Thanksgiving" when their minds are on football. Once more we live in a "peaceable kingdom"!

I know that deciding when to have Thanksgiving dinner (or dinner any day of the week) is not the world's most pressing problem to date. But such consideration is a simple indication that you know what is an important part of your life together and what is not. You know when your man is going to be all yours and when he is not. You *understand* that he has needs which have nothing to do with you. And if you can understand that about football, you can understand that about his business, his ambitions, his purposes—all those parts of his life in which you are not necessary!

Actually, "not being necessary" some of the time can be a boon! All those times now belong to you alone to do with as you like. You can turn your time and attention to your own talents, decide on your day, whether you want to work or play. At the very least, you can get the Christmas cards done early!

What did I tell you?! If you can understand football, you can understand men! Play the game good!

9
The Sadness of Separation

I wish there were no such word as *separation*. The very sound of it suggests sorrow and a shadow of loneliness falls across the face. Within the word there is the pain of divided parts that once were whole.

But *separation* is a word. It comes into Christian conversation. It cannot be wished away. Pretending there are no problems would be foolish and terribly, terribly unfair to those who loved, and for a time at least, have lost each other.

I do not know any answers. I know people. I have talked with women who were experiencing the personal pain of separation. I have seen how some of them have walked through it. I can only tell you what I've seen and heard and how I wish it were.

In the great majority of cases, especially among Christians, separation seems to be simply a matter of not being strong enough to stay when going would be easier. Christian psychologists say that when Christian couples separate there is usually no outside lover for either partner. There is simply a loss of care and communication, and soon it is easier to part than to stay together.

In such a case, what is the Christian wife to do? What is

her biblical guidance from God when her husband leaves her alone? *It is that she is still married.* The same is true for the Christian husband when a wife moves out of their home or out of their bed. He is still married! The sadness is just the same, the heartbreak just as hard! And perchance it is even more difficult for the husband who has been left alone to accept the challenge of God's guidance to remain married. But this book is about women—what women have confided and confessed to me—so we will look at separation through *their* windows.

The first reaction to being left alone is rage, mixed with desperation. This is the most dangerous time of all to take action. Do not plunge headlong into any decision and certainly not the decision to divorce. Separation may solve a multitude of situations you thought could never be solved.

A woman in our church works as an executive secretary in a large legal firm. She tells me that 80 percent of the people who divorce in the heat of anger, hurt, and humiliation later *wish* they had not done so. If the divorces were not final, there would be attempts, at least, to come to terms with the partners from whom they separated. (Certainly there are times when a partner *insists* on definite divorce instead of separation.) But if there is simply a severing of the togetherness, then wait. Wait. Pray for patience. Ask for an attitude of forgiveness and faith. Seek understanding of him and of yourself and of your situation. You can't know how often the waiting will make a difference in your fate.

When we were young, there was in our circle of "nearest and dearest," a couple who was so attractive, the all-American ideal. He had been the college football captain, she the cheerleader. Their children, two girls and a boy, were bright and beautiful. He was on the threshold of a vice-presidency at a bank. She was an officer in the Junior League and president of their couples Sunday School class.

One morning, after a decade of marriage, he entered the dining room with a small bag. "I must leave," he said. "I must get away. Marriage is too much for me." It was the only explanation he ever gave. True, they had married young, and perhaps he had missed some "free" years. True, there were frustrations with the family, children approaching the "terrible teens." True, there were some financial failures. *Also true*, he could have, should have, asked for the inner resources that only God can give, received them, and carried out his obligations. But, for one reason or another, he did not do this. He left.

His wife walked through the depths of despair. She wept. She lost weight. Her family worried. And then her courage and faith and fortitude took over. She gathered her strength together and stood with her head held high. She continued to go to her clubs and her church. She continued to sustain the children. She even took a part-time position at the church to fill her time to overflowing.

Meanwhile, as with Job, her "friends" rallied round! "He has money," they said. "Get him into a divorce court and clean him out!"

"He is my husband," she would say.

"Don't let him in the door," they counseled. "If he wants to come back, it should be begging on bloody knees!"

"This is his home," she would say.

The husband, living alone in a small apartment near the bank building, always received invitations to special occasion dinners: Christmas, Thanksgiving, Easter, the children's birthdays. There was no pressure. His place was set. Most often he came. Sometimes he did not. But his place was set. Often on Saturdays, he would drop by to repair the fence posts or to fertilize the flowers. But if he did not, for weeks at a time, there was no "discouraging word" from the wife.

"Doesn't it crush you," friends would ask, "to see him, to

104 A Woman's Song

be near him, and not to touch him, . . . to remember that he *left* you, . . . that he doesn't live here anymore?!"

"Yes," the wife would admit, "when I remember, it hurts very much!"

"Then *why* do you prolong it?! Why not make a break that is clean? Then the hurts can begin to heal!"

"That is not my right," she would say. "I married a man. I still love *that* man. And I married him for better or for worse. Right now, it's for worse. But my vow is the same, whether in bad times or in good." Her friends, including me, would marvel and then shake their heads at the hopelessness of the matter.

But one day he came to dinner to celebrate some accomplishment the children had made. He had been gone for several years, and the children were older—one of them in college. Early in the evening the young people left for their own engagements, and the husband went upstairs to fix a minor plumbing problem. Sometime later, wondering where he was, the wife followed him. She found him standing quietly in the bathroom door, holding in his hand an old purple toothbrush.

"My toothbrush," he said. "It was still on the shelf."

"It's still good," she replied.

He lifted his head and looked into her eyes for the care and encouragement he sought. "I should be with my toothbrush, don't you think?" He smiled uncertainly.

Her hands closed over his, still holding the toothbrush. There were no accusations, no recriminations, no wounding words. There was only the warmth of welcome for the man she had married, for better or for worse.

That was fifteen years ago. Though we no longer live in the same town, we have seen them on several occasions over the years. Each time they seem younger, more in love, and more successful because the wife was willing to wait! Like Job, she has had her life returned to her in full measure and more. There are not only children but also grandchildren to love. All the rewards of life she can share with him because she was willing to wait. She is a special inspiration to everyone who knows of her ever*lasting* love!

I know, honestly, that for every story which has a happy ending, there are a dozen more which do not. But if yours could be *one* of those happy endings, wouldn't it be worth it to wait? Wait, and ask God's guidance. He will be with you!

10
Dealing with Divorce

There was a movie about it, *Divorce American Style*. What used to be looked upon as the foremost failure in personal relationships is now seen only as a passing inconvenience. One out of every ten married Americans will be divorced before this year is finished. The statistics say this is a 300 percent increase from 1960! And you thought *inflation* was frightening!

Family counseling and care has become a billion-dollar business, and Christian churches everywhere are searching desperately for ways to save the sanctity of marriage. Most religious leaders feel that a lack of *prayer* and *preparation* (both in the selection of a mate and also in the concept of what makes a marriage) is a primary problem leading to divorce. The Roman Catholic Church is a denomination that has repeatedly denounced the practice of divorce. In numerous dioceses throughout the country now, a six months waiting period is required of any Catholic couple requesting marriage. During that time the prospective spouses are taught intensively through counseling courses. The Reverend Riley of the San Francisco Archdiocese commented on the purpose of the plan, "I spent twelve years preparing to be a priest," he said, "and it is harder to be a husband! We must prepare these young men!" The Catholic Church is only one of a number of denominations that are intent upon counseling their couples, now as never!

It *is* harder to be a husband than a priest! Indeed, being a husband, a wife, a marriage mate, is harder than most anything else on earth! It is harder than being a missionary. Missionaries get furloughs. It is harder than being a soldier. Soldiers get leaves and then they muster out! It is *much* harder than being a secretary! Secretaries are supposed to work certain hours and they get sick pay! But marriage lasts 24 hours a day, 365 days a year! Marriage, as God meant it to be, lasts for life! Like the wedding ring, a golden band with no beginning or end, marriage is forever! Both people should pray earnestly *before* marriage, to be assured that the mate is God's choice. And both people should pray earnestly *after* marriage, to find and follow God's will. If that is done, then according to God's theory the marriage will be the lasting relationship it should be. That is the *ideal*. We all recognize that the real world, made up of mortals, is not ideal. And divorce does come to Christian couples.

Divorce used to be done with much delay. It was a difficult experience and painfully expensive. Now it is "no fault," and in many cases you can do it yourself. It sounds so simple. But it is not God's first choice for his children.

Let me say at this point that I fully appreciate the fact that there are special people with special problems. I am not suggesting that a woman (or a man either, for that matter) "submit" to a situation that is damaging to physical or mental health. What I am suggesting is that committed Christian couples look beyond human laws, which offer the easy dissolution of marriages, to the laws of God.

According to Matthew 5:32, only our unfaithfulness

breaks the bonds of marriage. God's laws mean that most marriages should not be dissolved. In a world of words like *easy out, loophole language, I want,* and *my way,* we are often too ready to accept human solutions to a situation instead of God's. Incompatibility is simply not enough to dissolve a marriage. Nor is unhappiness. Nor is conflict or confusion. One husband will have temperamental moods. Another will be crude and critical at times. One wife will be careless in her personal appearance, another rude, another too sharp with her words. These and many more problems like them are not easy to live with or to love, but they are not grounds for divorce, not by God's laws anyway. And God's laws are the laws Christians should live by.

God's laws are the laws Christians *should* live by. But Christians are sometimes carnal. I have seen fine young husbands left alone because young women were too attached to mother. I have seen beautiful young wives abandoned because handsome young men suddenly felt they must "find themselves." I have seen older women, after a lifetime in a relationship, alone because their middle-aged men selfishly turned to someone younger in a last attempt to salvage youth. I have seen families left without a father because some man cannot *be* a man and cope with the pressures of being a parent. I have seen women leap from one marriage to another over nothing more than a lack of money, wanting a husband number two who can give them more of the luxuries of life than husband number one. These cases are not hypothetical examples. I have seen *Christians* involved in all of the above.

Christians do divorce, so divorce must be dealt with. It is devastating. It is like amputation. The wounds are deep. The church can be a haven for the newly divorced man or woman so in need of friendship and sharing. Also, Christian counseling can give assurance that life does go on and that the process can be productive. There should be no shame at this time in asking for and receiving both mental and physical help.

But as always, the spiritual part of a person, the soul in need of solace, will be fed most effectively by the Word. This was God's purpose in giving the Bible to us! There is a chapter in Isaiah that I love because it proves more than any other passage that God knew about broken hearts. It is literally like loving arms being placed around you as you read. It is applicable to the woman who waits patiently through a separation and also to the woman who has already known the devastation of a divorce which, for one reason or another, could not be avoided. It is beautiful to the barren woman who did not bear children at all or who lost her children, either through death, separation, or because they wandered away from the Lord's love.

The passage was written to Zion, as a promise of redemption. But it is also written to women. It has all the sweet assurance for which feminine hearts have yearned through the years. I love especially the translation from *The Amplified Bible* of Isaiah 54. Every line is soothing; every line is like healing balm for the hurting, lines like, "For the Lord has called you like a woman forsaken, grieved in spirit and heartsore, even a wife [wooed and won] in youth, when she is later refused and scorned, says your God. For a brief moment I forsook you, but with great compassion and mercies I gather you to Me again. . . . This is as the days of Noah to Me; as I have sworn that the waters of Noah should no more go over the earth, so have I sworn that I will not be angry with you or rebuke you. For though the mountains should depart and the hills be shaken or removed, yet My love and kindness shall not depart from you, nor shall My covenant of peace and completeness be removed, . . . O you afflicted, storm-tossed and not comforted, behold, I will set your stones in fair colors

. . . and lay your foundations with sapphires" (vv. 6-11).

Has there ever been a more beautiful display of tenderness? Not only does he promise peace but precious jewels as well! You can live! By God's grace and God's goodness, you can live!

11
Masterpiece

Some couples make masterpieces of their marriages, works of art, the *Master's* works of art!

The hopeless heart asks, "After love has left, what is there?" The Christian couple answers, "There is commitment!" And I, for one, believe that *this* is even more meaningful to a relationship than romance! (Surely there is no reason there cannot be both. Romance and commitment are, actually, separate colors of the same rainbow.)

But we need to be realistic. Most women have days when they don't love their husbands, at least not romantically. And there will be days when husbands don't love their wives. There may be days and DAYS when you don't love each other.

There may be some exceptional couples who have *always* been *in* love. I can think of one or two such couples in our circle of friends who seem to be so suited to each other that there is no conflict or confusion. (Or maybe they are just nicer, more knowledgeable, or more mature than the rest of us.) But believe me, they are the exceptions to the rule. Most mortals are hard to live with. They have habits and moods and emotions that are not lovable. Sometimes the dark side of us and our loved ones seem to overshadow the light side, and we feel that "love" has left. What we have to sustain us is commitment. For a time that may be *all* we have, and thus the relationship is still meaningful!

A popular song says, "Love is so divine, Now that you are mine." If indeed love is divine, then I submit to you that *commitment* makes it so. God himself showed us how to love. "I will be with you always," he said. "I will never leave you." He took the church as his beloved bride. The church is sometimes loving and easy to live with and sometimes not. But God said, "You are mine, and nothing on this earth, or above the earth, or below the earth, nothing will ever separate you from me!" He has made a commitment to us. *That* is love so divine! It was meant to be a pattern for his people, especially his people in love.

The delight, of course, is that love is the most resilient emotion! It may lie dormant, but true love, given and received by trusting individuals, does not die. And the second blooming, or the third or the fourth, is often the most glorious of all. It's a lot to look forward to, like waiting through winter believing always in the blooms of spring!

Why, then, do so many husbands and wives not wait together for a second blooming of love? Because as a world, we have lost the *image* of marriage. It used to be the sweet mystery of life. Now it is common knowledge, with the emphasis on *common*. Brides once wore white. Grooms were nervous. Marriage was new from the "first night" until "forever after."

But now nothing seems new or forever. The idea of "free love" changed the way many people think about love and marriage. If ever there were a lie in the world, it is "free love." Love is never free. Never, ever! Sex is sometimes free for the moment. (Later there may be much to pay in either guilt or grief.) But love is never free. Love is many things, all of them filled with precious promises, but "free" is not one of them! True, trusting love *costs* you everything, *everything*, as you give yourself in love for life to another.

Popular books, magazines, television shows, and movies seem to say that all men must want many women. How else would they prove they are marvelous lovers? Thank heaven, however, there *are* some sensitive men left, even in Hollywood. I recall a memorable night on "The Johnny Carson Show," as Carson bantered with his pal and tennis partner, Ricardo Montalban. "And how," asked Carson, with that little boy leer that has made him a legend, "do you like being a Latin lover?"

Montalban, easily the most handsome man in the movies and certainly one of the most sensitive, replied seriously, "Oh, John, what a thin phrase that is, 'Latin lover'! Any man alive can jump in and out of bed. That doesn't take any talent. *Boys* can do it! But it takes a *man* to keep one woman happy for thirty years! That takes talent and tenderness and fiery finesse that most men never know! My wife is all women to me. She is different every day. I would no more want another woman than I would want another heart! I have made her happy, and *that* is the difference between a man and a Latin lover!"

Oh, hooray for our side! I have admired Ricardo Montalban ever since.

Lately, women too have been told that they should not be shy about wanting many men: be liberated in love! I did not realize how many people had this attitude until recently. A woman I do not know well worked with me on a civic committee. I think I was as close to a Christian as she had ever come. She was fascinated. Was I really good? Did I really want to be? Her questions were endless. She found my answers incredulous.

Finally one day she figured me out to her satisfaction. It was toward the end of the time we worked together, and I was tense and tired. "Joy!" she said suddenly. "Stop being gracious and good. It's making you nervous! You know, you wouldn't be nearly so nervous if you'd have an affair now and then!"

We both laughed, but I could see that she was more serious than not. My life was unnatural to her. (*Supernatural* is actually the word for the Christian life, but the world sees it as unnatural.) She looked at me and laughed. How could I limit myself to one man? Why would I want to? It was beyond belief! Oh, what words could I have used to tell her about the depth, the deep desire, the meaning of a life-lasting love? I wanted so much for her to look at more than *surface* life! Alas! The lady and I were having a conversation about different subjects.

If, as with that woman, you do not understand marriage, you will not understand *me* at this moment. What I am writing will be like a foreign language to you and a little frightening. You will not like it in the least! But though you may fret or be frivolous about that which you do not understand, even as you smile your worldly-wise smile, you will wonder in your heart of hearts if there is a level of life somewhere that you are missing, a dimension where you can never be because you are blinded to it.

If, on the other hand, you have known what it is like to share so deeply with someone that you do not distinguish his desires from yours, you will understand me. You will remember those mornings when you woke to a world that held only him, knowing that he sensed the same thing. There was the wonderful letting go of *you* and the becoming *us*. Moments like these in a marriage may be frequent, or they may be few, depending on the people involved. But if ever once you have known such a blending of body, soul, and spirit, you will understand what I am writing. That kind of blending can never come from "living together" or "affairs" or even *loving*. That kind of completeness comes only in a marriage that combines love and commitment, a marriage that has been polished through the years and the tears and the testing!

Picture the sculptor who is about to begin a work of art. He is surrounded by many beautiful blocks of marble, and he wants them all! He begins a statue, the face, the eyes, the lips, the torso, but suddenly he is tired. He leaves the work unfinished and moves on. Another beautiful block of marble, another statue begun, but the proportions are harder to fashion than he had first thought. Again he leaves the work unfinished and moves on. He begins another and another and another. He leaves each work after a little while. In one, the design is too difficult. In another, he finds the marble flawed; it would take too long to polish the flaws away. Another time he feels suddenly that he was only infatuated with this one. He doesn't really like it now, why finish? And so on and on and on! At the end of his "career," he sits surrounded by bits and pieces of art. Not one completed masterpiece! Wasted time, wasted talent, wasted life!

But across the way another sculptor works. He chooses the marble most suited to his way of working. It is durable, as well as beautiful. He designs carefully. Then he begins to create. He gives attention to detail. When he is tired, he reminds himself of what the finished work will be, and he is renewed. Finally he lays down his tools and begins to polish. Over and over again he refines the finished work. Finally he is done, and before him is a magnificent work of art, a masterpiece! Inspired, and now inspiring for all who admire it!

This is the difference between a series of surface affairs and a marriage. The first results in bits and pieces. The second is a masterpiece. It was not made in a day, but during a lifetime. It was sometimes tedious. It was sometimes difficult. It was sometimes a duty. But the result was a masterpiece!

What the world does not understand is that the artist who makes the masterpiece does it for his own delight and love! He could never, ever be satisfied with bits and pieces. Nobody forces him to finish the work! He does it because it gives him a pleasure that the world cannot comprehend!

It has always been a mystery to me why the world can understand the demanding dedication of a musician, an artist, an athlete, or a scientist but cannot understand the consecration of a Christian. An artist in any area gives his whole life to his work. He is consumed by it! I am amazed each time the Van Cliburn Piano Competition is held in Fort Worth, Texas, to hear the interviews with the young people who come from around the world. Many of them have been playing and composing since they were children, and all of them practice at the piano some six to eight hours a day! The interviews with the young people of the Olympics are the same! Those who skate and ski and bend their bodies with such precision on the bars never miss a day in practice, and it has been so with them since they were children.

But let us work on our Christian lives from childhood, let us pray daily and practice our faith, and let us do whatever we must to make marriages secure and sanctified, and the world cannot comprehend. Of *course* it takes discipline and denial of self. *Certainly* there are days we don't want to do it! But oh, the thrill of it! And the peace of it! And the pleasure of it! And the wonder of a marriage that warms you and strengthens you and excites you for . . . *life*! A masterpiece!

I've said a lot of things in this book about love that women already know. (It's the men who sometimes don't know, and *they* aren't going to be reading this book!)

So I have written these chapters simply *to let you know you're not alone!* To let you know that there are women everywhere who have been through similar situations and survived! Knowing that others have stood strong, kept their commitments, and abided by their responsibilities gives you confidence for your future. By the same token, you who have been successful in all these areas will be witnesses to others. This is one of the best reasons for being "true-blue," the encouragement it offers to others. "If she can do it, I can do it," they who see you will say; and you will have saved not only yourself but also someone else from falling in the face of overwhelming odds.

Don't we all follow-the-leader a lot anyway? One summer Drew Ann and I were invited to watch the filming of the television movie *Skyward* being made at a small airport nearby. It happened during the Dallas heat wave, when temperatures reached 110 degrees for several days. Drew Ann and I arrived at the little airport laden with a supply of pink lemonade and sun lotion. The scene that day was done out on the concrete runway, which by four o'clock felt like a skillet over an open fire. Cameramen and crew wore wet towels around their necks, which were resoaked in ice water every few minutes. Everyone was blistered as a beet and looked ready to drop down and die, all except the most important person there. Miss Bette Davis, that legendary lady of Hollywood, moved through her paces as patiently as if she were shooting on an air-conditioned sound stage, take, after take, after take. I watched her in wonder, as the landscape literally waved before my face. *She has to be seventy if she's a day,* I thought. *If she can stand it, surely I can stand it!* And so we stayed for a truly remarkable performance! Any other day I would have fainted dead away or left to lie down or both. But somehow the sun did not seem so overwhelming that day. Bette Davis could stand the heat! Why not me?

Do you see the importance of standing strong? It is not only for yourself but also for others! A friend and I were discussing those "terrible times" in marriage. "Joy," she said, "I'm not the actress you are. You are a professional image-maker, and you carry that over into your personal life, always presenting the 'right' image. I can't do that! I won't! When I'm hurt or unhappy, I show it. I feel I should! Don't you feel dishonest pretending 'all's well,' when really 'it's not'?"

I had to smile at her. But my answer was serious, "Living a lie? Oh, no, never! I am living the *truth* that God's 'grace is sufficient' (2 Cor. 12:9), 'I can do all things through Christ' (Phil. 4:13), Love 'suffereth long, . . . seeketh not her own, . . . beareth all things, believeth all things' (1 Cor. 13:4-7)! I have never been so *honest* in my life!"

You can be, you see, a glowing example of that all-sufficient grace, of the victory and the vindication of your efforts, of the fact that God's way works! *That* is not a lie. That is the Word in glorious technicolor! And how priceless the reward when you have won, when the precious moments return to your marriage, when the rain lifts and the sunlight bursts upon you and yours, beautiful and bright! It was for this day that you endured!

How many times you have wailed, "But I don't know how to *take* him!" You already have, my dear! Wasn't it at the wedding that you said, "I take thee, to be my lawful wedded husband, to have and to hold from this day forward, in sickness and in health, in poverty and in wealth, for better or for worse"? Yes, you did! And so did I! I take my darling husband, and in return, I give myself.

Section III
The Joyful Song
of Living and Learning

Christian antiquity claimed a most enlightened man named Augustine, whose written works are considered the noblest of his time. Augustine believed that to learn mentally, physically, and especially spiritually, was humankind's great service to God. Only in learning can we find and follow God fully, he felt. The search for learning is to be lifelong, ending only in eternity! The Christian's search for learning leads him to the garden, to the cross, and beyond to the crown. These were on the path of our Lord. He leads—and we follow.

On the Algerian coast of Africa, under Roman rule in AD 300, there lived a man named Augustine, who possessed the most powerful mind of his time. He became the philosopher of the age. He became also a believer in Christ. His probing intellect, coupled with deep devotion, led to profound enlightenment. Both biblical and secular scholars regard his writings as the greatest works of Christian antiquity other than the Bible itself.

Augustine was sure that the *service* of a Christian's life was to learn mentally and physically, but especially spiritually. He insisted that only through the learning process can we find and follow God completely. It must be, then, the consuming passion of the Christian to seek that part of ourselves that is made in "the image of God" (Gen. 1:27). This consuming passion for Augustine was lifelong. It did not confound him that he could never know all the answers. His search would be ended only in eternity. The fact that there were things he would never know on this earth only confirmed his faith in heaven. If God is God, then he is greater by far than anything humans can ever understand. We learn and learn and learn, and finally we accept him by simple faith!

God himself said as much, "For my thoughts are not your thoughts, neither are your ways my ways, . . . For as the heavens are higher than the earth, so are my ways higher than your ways, and my thoughts than your thoughts" (Isa. 55:8-9).

One morning Augustine walked beside the Mediterranean Sea. He saw a little lad digging diligently on the shore. The childish hands had made a shallow basin in the sand. It was to be an imaginary lake in which he would sail his make-believe boats. He had begun to dig a tiny trench toward the sea. A few feet more and he would reach the water.

Augustine sat down on the sand beside the boy. "You see," said the little lad, "soon I will be able to move the sea into my lake!" The great man smiled at the earnest misconception of the childish mind that one could move the sea into a shallow basin on the shore. *How like that child we are,* he thought, *to assume our minds could ever contain the countless thoughts of Almighty God!*

The desire to search for a Supreme Being is universal. On every continent, in every tribe on earth, there is something to represent a god, a divinity, and the people are religiously devoted to it. Persons who have been atheistic and have finally found God tell us that they daily and doggedly fought the experience of faith for years. With their minds they could not accept, yet with their hearts they continually wished for *a lord.*

There are theologians who believe that this universal search for a Supreme Being is proof enough that he is. The living body becomes thirsty and must drink to stay alive. This need presupposes the existence of water. The living body becomes hungry and must eat to stay alive. This need presupposes the existence of food. There is also within the human heart the inherent yearning to worship. This need presupposes the existence of God. To say no to the need for water and food means physical death. To say no to the need for God means spiritual death. So we search, first for God himself and then for our true selves made in "the image of God." What a precious promise when we read, "Seek, and ye shall find" (Matt. 7:7).

It is, of course, the nature of humans to want to *know.* Where? When? Why? We always ask. Why the death, the despair, the pain? Why the sunshine, the rain, the seasons? There will always be questions without answers. (Take, for instance, my ten-year-old son who asked, "Why did God bother to make a man in the first place, I mean, if God *knew* man was going to eat the apple and cause all this confusion? God *couldn't* have been *that* lonesome!" Now there, my friend, is a first-rate QUESTION!)

But God is God. He is not to be understood until eternity. He made heaven and earth and me; and my constant search for him, my constant learning about him and his will and his way, is my service to him!

The joyful song of living and learning is what constitutes the difference between life and death. When one ceases to learn, one dies. The body may be breathing, but the person within that body is no longer alive!

Life *is* learning. Christians can have the happiest, most exhilarating experiences possible, for their learning combines the spiritual as well as the intellectual and physical! Christians learn with "heart and soul," as well as with "head." Thus Christians face the future with untold promise! Their today is promising. Their tomorrow is promising. Their eternity is promising. A body and a brain will eventually cease to produce new cells. They will grow old. They will wither away. But the soul never stops learning, growing, living, never! And if that soul is saved, then there are all the glories of heaven to learn! Joyfully! Gladly! Forever!

12
Noble? Not Me!

Humans are just not naturally noble! We would like to be, but we are not. Human nature is filled with fault and has been ever since Eve gave Adam the "apple" and he ate it! That's why the Lord sent his Son to teach us how to live all over again. But just because we have accepted Christ, become Christians, been born again, does not mean that we are through with human nature! It is within us, conflicting with our spiritual nature constantly, and we will do well to be forewarned! This is precisely why the Bible says, "The fear of the Lord is the beginning of wisdom" (Ps. 110:10), for without that fear we would fall prey to our faults much more often than we do! Our good intentions can't be counted on. Nor does the knowledge of God's love for us keep us from waywardness. You would think that out of pure thankfulness to God's grace we would learn to live the good life he intends for us to live. But not so with human natures. Often, it is only the "fear" of the Lord that will deter us from manifold mistakes.

We are all susceptible to sin in many matters. Consider the matter of commitment for one. There are those in my life to whom I am committed out of lots of love, not duty. But often even love becomes a duty. (Anything that is day to day tends to seem like a duty at sometime or another.) At those times when we are weak, we might break those commitments were it not for the "fear" of the Lord!

For instance, I can be as tantalized by Camelot as the next lady. You remember Camelot! That never-never land of love and laughter where everyone was bright and beautiful! Queen Guinevere had King Arthur, his kingdom, and his love! What more could the lady want? But along came Lancelot, and she wanted him too! And she had him! Ah, such romance! And there was Robert Goulet singing, "If I could ever leave you," and Julie Andrews looking like an angel! Makes you want to throw commitment to the winds and run away with the first man who can sing!

But then there's that line from God's Word that says, "Thou shalt not commit adultery" (Ex. 20:14), and another that says the judgment of the Lord is swift and sure (Mal. 3:5). Suddenly Camelot seems like a dangerous place to be! I have visions of wandering in the wilderness for forty years, and all at once it makes sense to keep my commitments!

You see, I feel I have good reason to fear the Lord. He *made* me. He knows the number of hairs on my head. He holds my *life* in his hand. I love him. I want to learn about him. But it is not enough until I fear him! The Word says, this is the *beginning*!

Often, once we have *begun* our soul-searching, the first close encounter that a Christian has is with sin! I do not mean to say that non-Christians do not encounter sin, of course they do. But they look at it differently. Sin is something that they do or are doing, and they may even differentiate that it is wrong instead of right. Their main concern is, however, who will know or who will care and will they be caught, corrected, or made to "pay."

With the Christian, sin is something else. Sin is separation from fellowship with God. This is true even with the carnal Christian, and certainly for the Christian who wants a living relationship with the Lord. Sin in one's life brings about an immediate separation from peace in the presence of God. It is like shutting the door on daylight.

Now there are sins which we discuss in Sunday School. Have you been a gossip, a cheat? Have you smoked or eaten too much? Have you been a snob? Have you told a "little lie" somewhere, sometime, perhaps to protect someone's feelings or to cover a small mistake? We've all known some of these sins, certainly. They are "safe" subjects at Sunday School, and the only "sin" to which many will admit!

Some of God's people were told about Jesus as children and led to the Lord when they were young, when sins were the size of the children but they became aware of their sin of separation from God through the leading of the Holy Spirit. But whether you became a Christian in your childhood, or whether you were saved after you had walked the "way of the world," you are going to encounter sin and sins in your life. For some of God's people the sins will be the kind we hide from others, the kind we hide from ourselves, but, of course, not from God! Whether we say it is so or not, whether others see it or not, sin is there; and the separation from God tears our hearts apart.

Have any of you committed adultery? This is a question your Bible teacher might never ask during the course of a lesson, but don't dismiss it. There are Sunday School pupils who have, and some as lately as last week. Have you killed? is another question that is probably never asked. But *have* you? Perhaps not literally. Perhaps you have not taken breath from a body. But have you taken the light from someone's life? Have you crushed the sparkling spirit from a wife, a husband, a child, a parent, a friend, with your selfishness, your criticisms, your unreasonable rages? Have you stolen? Have you taken something from someone that was theirs, not yours, literally, without the law? Or was it legal when you stole a man's business, his house, or perhaps his profit? Do you indulge in drink or drugs? Have you led others to do so? Have you *allowed* others to do so—the family, the friend who has accepted the glass from your hand? Have you worshiped at the altar of other gods? There are many altars in this modern world: pride, prejudice, fame, fortune, self. Where have you worshiped lately? Have you worshiped at all?

These are questions that will probably not come to you on Sunday morning, but may come to mind in the still of the night, in the darkness when no one is listening but you and the Lord. And sooner or later they will have to be settled. For the Christian, whether carnal or committed, simply cannot survive separation from God.

Explanations as to why Christians sin can be several, such as we are human; temptation is too powerful; we fall under the influence of the world; we're in a rat race and the rats are winning. All of these explanations are pointless. We *sin* because *Satan* is in the world, is the powerful prince of this world, and because, more than any other force in this world, he is the source of conflict and confusion, most *especially* in the spirit of the Christian. There was a famous television comedian who used to say of his "wicked ways," "The devil made me do it!" The truth of that statement is staggering! Turn to 1 Peter 5:8 and see for yourself! We could never, ever stand courageous, conquering, in our own strength. Only with God's help could we ever hope for victory. And because we often depend upon our own strength, we sin. When we sin, Satan has won, for his goal is to separate us continually from Christ.

But the Christian will not stay separated simply because

we cannot stand to be in that state. We will realize, sooner or later, the magnitude of our sin, and we will come to grips with it as we must. We will repent, fall on our faces before God, and ask forgiveness. This is the *first* step toward reconciliation with the Lord, and most of us will eventually take that first step! It is with the *second* step that many of us fail most miserably. That second step is to *accept* God's forgiveness! Many men and women fail to accept God's forgiveness (just as many fail to accept his salvation) simply because they cannot understand it or see it clearly. Actually we fail to forgive *ourselves*! *Logically* we can accept God's forgiveness, for we know this to be his nature. But *literally* we cannot, for we feel we have done something that is unforgivable, according to the world. (Indeed, we may still be suffering from the corrosive stains of that sin. A simple illustration is the man who stops smoking finally, after forty years, but his body is still suffering the stifled lungs that are the result of smoking.) Just because we have repented, prayerfully and completely, does not mean that we will not suffer the consequences of sin. This is simply a law of nature, the natural course of things. It has nothing to do with whether we have been forgiven by God. Still we frequently see our sin as unforgivable.

Mortals accept more readily what they can see than what they cannot see. They cannot *see* the forgiveness of God. But they can *see* the hurt and the harm that results from their sin, to themselves, and to others. They can see the love forever lost and the lasting scars that come because of their sin. Therefore, they refuse the forgiveness of God, if not with their minds then with their hearts. They continue to bear the burden of guilt and grief, sometimes even to the grave. They have thus paralyzed their relationship with the Lord, for they have closed their veins to the ventilating flow of "the blood of the Lamb." Christ's blood was shed so that he might be our

Savior, not only in *death* but also in *life!* How sad that there are those who fail to accept his blood, not only for eternal salvation but also for their day-to-day salvation!

In both salvation and forgiveness, *faith* is the key word. We are saved through faith, and we are forgiven through faith. We don't have to see it or understand it, just accept it, for it is so. The Bible tells me so. God loves. God forgives. Those are facts. And once the forgiveness of God is accepted (no matter the magnitude of the sin of the suffering) then the door is opened again on the daylight!

Rahab was a harlot. She became a believer. She was not only forgiven but she was also an ancestor of Christ. David committed adultery. He repented. He was not only forgiven but he also became the conquering king of Israel. Moses committed murder. He confessed. He was not only forgiven but he also led God's chosen people to the threshold of the Promised Land. Peter denied Christ the night before the cross. He was not only forgiven but he was also presented with "the keys of the kingdom" (Matt. 16:19). And then there was the adulteress about to be stoned! "He that is without sin among you, let him first cast a stone," said the Lord! She was a woman whose sin was unforgivable to the world but not to the Savior (John 8:7)!

These people did not go without punishment. But the separation from God, from his blessing and his bounty, *ended* when they asked for, received, and accepted his forgiveness! Oh, the forgiveness of God! It is unfathomable, so far above and beyond anything we ask or seek for! God forgives us because he is fair. God forgives us because he does not want to lose us to himself or to his service. God forgives us because he had promised to hear the prayer of the sin-sick soul. But mostly, God forgives us because he loves us, deeply, devotedly, divinely; and nothing we will ever do will take away his tender, longing, lasting love for us! Thank God!

A poignant page from our national history will always be the one written during the hostage crisis in Iran during 1978 and 1979. After 444 days the American men and women for whom the world had been so concerned were freed. As we watched their happy homecoming, their buoyant, boisterous welcome, the nation was collectively humming a little tune, "Tie a yellow ribbon round the old oak tree." The inspiration for that song was supposedly a story published in *The New York Post* in 1971, in an article written by the award-winning columnist, Pete Hamill. And perhaps that *is* the story that the songwriters saw. But long before Pete Hamill was a columnist and long before Tony Orlando was singing songs, my mother was telling a version of that story to me as an illustration of the love and forgiveness of God.

Mother's story came from the days of the Great Depression (a time with which my parents were well acquainted, for they were students at Southwestern Seminary during those days of destitution for the entire population).

In November of 1930 the bare, bleak lands of West Texas had never looked so desolate, as a single train, made up of a few creaky cars, whistle-stopped its way across the range. A cold, gray day was turning into a cold, gray twilight, and inside the passenger car there were only two people: an elderly minister near the back and a young man near the front. The young man wore clothing that was clean but frayed and worn like the worried look on his face. Finally the old minister moved forward to sit beside him.

"Son," he said, "I'm a preacher of the Word, and I've learned, in my life, how to listen! Would you like to tell me why you are so worried?"

Tears began to roll down the rough young cheeks, as the boy began to talk. "I left home, oh, it seems like a lifetime ago, that I left home! And I left behind me all I'd been taught: the good Book, the preachin', and the prayin'. I tried to live without it! I thought I could! But I got into trouble—terrible, terrible trouble—and finally found myself in jail. It broke my mother's heart, Reverend, just broke her heart with me in jail. She cried and cried, I know she did because, when her letters came, the words would be all smeared with tears. I could see the sadness was weighin' on her. I thought it best if she forgot about me. And so I sent the last letters back unopened, like I didn't want them.

"But, oh, Reverend, I've changed my mind. I'm free now, and I want more than anything I can think of to go home. But maybe *she* doesn't want *me* now! Maybe she can't forgive me! After what I've done, I'd understand if she didn't want me to stay, you know!

"So I wrote her a letter last week, and I told her I was gettin' out! This train passes by our old home place, the farm, the house, the barn, and out back behind the barn there's this old oak tree where I used to climb up high and wave to the engineers as the trains went by. Well, Reverend, I told my ma, 'I'll be on the 6:30 train next Sunday, passing by our place. And if maybe you could let me come home, if maybe you could forgive me, then tie a white handkerchief to one of the branches of that old oak tree behind the barn. If it's there, I'll get off at the station and come on home. But if it's not, I'll just keep on riding, into the night!'

"That's what I told her, Reverend. That's what I told my ma. It's not far now, just around the next hill up there, and we should be able to see it!"

The old preacher sat, praying silently, as the young man strained forward to see through the gathering dusk. And then they both gasped out loud! The train rounded the hill! And there was the little farm—the house, the pasture, the barn! But it was the old oak tree that lighted up the landscape, for from every branch from top to bottom there hung not a handkerchief but a *bedsheet,* waving in the wind, welcoming a wayward boy.

And as my mother would tell me this story, always weeping a bit, she would say, "And this is like God's love, and God's great forgiveness, toward us!"

Ah, we do fail because we are frail or because sin was too strong a temptation or because we are worn away with everyday worries and tasks and toils. Suddenly we find that we have wandered so far away!

"God, can you forgive me? God, do you love me? Lord, if you love me, send me a sign!"

"A sign? My child, I have sent you my *Son!*"

To believe in sin alone would be to accept *death.* But to believe in sin *and the Savior* is to accept *life,* today, tomorrow, everlasting!

One more observation needs to be made about sin and our society today. It has become increasingly popular to label sin as sickness and thus dismiss the need for an admission of sin and the repentance necessary for forgiveness! This is an observation which I perceived personally, but other people have come to the same conclusion. One of our church members here at First Baptist, Dallas, is the famous motivationalist Zig Zigler. His seminars are not only informative but also fun, and he has several classic examples of the "loose" labels people put on sin!

One of the best is the story of the wife married to the abusive husband whose drinking had been diagnosed as a "sickness." This "sickness" caused him, on occasion, to come home with the temperament of a raging bull, beat his wife

unmercifully, and then pass out. Upon receiving one especially bad beating, the wife decided "enough is enough."
While her husband lay impassive in his "passed out" stage,
she took a razor strap and beat him on his back from head to
toe until he was bloody. When he regained consciousness he
could hardly believe his condition. He was a candidate for the
nearest hospital and possibly plastic surgery to replace the
skin on his back! Standing over him was his placid wife who
said, "And if you ever beat me again, *next* time I will turn you
over and do this to the *front* of you!" Reportedly, the man's
"sickness" was cured completely! She had beaten the devil out
of him, quite literally!

This story is told as an "unusual" case, of course (and it is
not meant to minimize the fact of effective medical treatment
for any social sickness, treatment that is often a saving
resource)! But the *point* remains the same. We often excuse
sin as sickness!

I have known men who had tempers almost this terrible
when they were completely sober. They were dangerous to
themselves and to those around them, and they were called
"sick." Actually, they were simply sour at the world and took it
out on those nearest and dearest to them. A terrible temper is
not the only sin, by far, that is labeled politely "sickness."

The person who *lies* with serious intent can be just as
dangerous, perhaps more so, than the person with the terrible
temper. (At least the danger from a raging bull is out in the
open.) But a lie can be so subtle that often the damage is not
discovered until it is too late. Lies are told for lots of reasons in
the beginning. The person who cannot bear to be wrong will
lie to "save face." The person who is afraid of failure will lie to
save his job. The person who must always make "an impression" will lie about his bank account, his car, or his career. If
the lie to save face must hurt or harm another, it does not

matter. If the lie to save the job must point the finger unjustly at another, it does not matter. If the lie to make an impression must be malicious, it does not matter.

Finally, the lying has taken place so long that the person does not know the difference between the truth and a lie. Only the "end" is important, never the "means." It is at this point that the lying is labeled "pathological" and the person is called *sick*. Actually, he is simply bearing false witness against those with whom he works and lives and loves. God has said, "Thou shalt not bear false witness" (Ex. 20:16). You see, it is sin. While the bearer of false witness may, indeed, need Christian counseling, that person also needs to repent!

There are numerous other such sins that have been mislabeled, and this is the greatest disservice we can do sinners (or ourselves, if *we* are the sinners)! In the lives of people who are plagued with such problems, there has often never been anyone who cared enough to point to this tendency for sin. It has been allowed to grow. They continue to unleash whatever form of hurt or humiliation their sin takes until finally they are bound up with it, completely caught up with it, their reason lost. They have not only been sick but also sinful, but we have politely relieved them of the need for the acceptance of their sin and the repentance necessary for their forgiveness!

Recognizing this fact can go a long way toward preserving the sanity of not only the sinner but also of the circle of family and friends with whom he lives. It can also go a long way in planning the approach to the person with the problem. A sick person, seriously sick, needs a different kind of help than a sinful person. An oversimplification would be to say one needs pills, and the other needs prayer (and perhaps a spiritual spanking)!

But never is it so simple. Each case is as complex as the

personality involved. It is vital that each is examined painstakingly so that the proper treatment can be applied. Whether the problem is within yourself or within one near and dear to you, be certain that out of a sense of love or pity you do not mislabel the situation. Seek God's aid through prayer. He will direct you!

Novelist John Steinbeck's *East of Eden* was an epic of the passionate emotions of two blood brothers, one good, the other bad from birth. The book was symbolic of the biblical brothers, Cain and Abel. There is a scene in which a Chinese servant seeks enlightenment as to the evil that is in man and to learn whether or not it can be controlled. Repeatedly he pours over the story of Cain and Abel, the first contrasts in good and evil among men. Finally, he finds a phrase that gives him the satisfaction he seeks. God speaks to Cain, a man whose dark nature is manifest, and declares to Cain his clear choices, "The sin at your door desires you, but 'thou shalt rule over' him" (see Gen. 4:7). Translated into the Chinese phraseology, the verse seemed to say to the Chinese servant, "The sin at your door desires you, but thou *mayest* overrule." It was not the word used to denote doubt—perhaps you will, perhaps you won't. It was the word used when granting permission! You *may* choose! God grants us the *permission* to make the choice, good or evil, light or darkness, life or death!

The Chinese servant was satisfied. There was hope. Evil can be controlled. We need not be sacrificed to sinful natures!

13
Refined by Fire

I was half a century old before I realized that *everyone*, each and everyone on earth, has sorrow. I am a trusting soul, and I tend to take people at their word. When people told me they were terrific, I believed. Years later into life, I finally realized that *nobody* is totally terrific! They may be at peace in the midst of their peril, they may be fighting the conflict and winning, they may be the most marvelous witness alive to the power and presence of the Lord! But nobody is totally terrific! Everybody has sorrow!

Sorrow can be private, or it can be public. Sometimes I think public sorrow is so much easier to bear. When a loved one lies dying, your Christian friends rally round with food, money, and prayer support. When your house burns down, they bring you table lamps and boxes of sheets and towels. When an automobile accident leaves you in traction, they send flowers and funny cards. When a son or daughter is wayward, they give you sympathy. But there are times when your heart breaks silently for some reason you cannot tell. Perhaps you feel you must be silent to protect another person's privacy. Perhaps it is that *you* must suffer silently to save someone *else* from suffering. Perhaps it is simply that there is no need for anyone else to know. But when burdens cannot be shared with friends and loved ones, we feel lonely. The old Negro spiritual caught the soul's cry in the words, "Nobody knows the trouble I've seen! Nobody knows but Jesus"! That, of course, is our salvation, *that Jesus knows,* and in the end it is enough. But it doesn't keep life in such a situation from being lonely.

Time and time again I have been shocked anew at learning of the secret, lonely sorrow of this person or that. How often have I thought, *She is such a positive person, surely she is never down!* Or *he is so successful, surely he is never doubtful!* Or *my Sunday School teacher is perfect, surely she is never tempted or tested or tried as I am!* Wrong! The happiest woman you know may weep every day—weep and pray and prevail upon God—and then get up to go about her business, once more the picture of the blessed and the beautiful Christian. She has conquered her cross, yes, but she pays the price and does it alone. ALONE. Such people are the unsung soldiers of the cross! No one but Jesus knows what it has taken and will continue to take, each and every day, for these people to accomplish what seems so simple!

Some people are aided by Christian psychologists or prayer-and-share groups, or mutual emotional therapy. Others must be alone with the Lord. I, for instance, cannot "strip" emotionally. I cannot. There is pain, overpowering emotional pain in my life, for I have sorrow just as you, and you, and you. People hurt me, I am distressed and distraught, and I face defeat. And so sometimes there is pain that I would not share with anyone in the world, not my husband or my children or my mother or my closest confidant. I am not silent because I am *naturally* silent. (You know that I am not.) I am not silent because I am ashamed or guilty or proud or prejudiced. It is not because I am trying to protect anyone, not even me. It is simply that I *cannot*. No more than I can open my head and show you my brain, can I open my heart and show you that particular pain. It is sometimes so deep, dark, and consuming inside me that only God can see. Only God can separate me from it and deal with it divinely. There is no human help.

But, hallelujah, there is heavenly help, when you need it, where you need it, how you need it! And when you have found it to be sufficient (and you will), you will know that there is no more splendid, spiritual blessing! It is the balm of Gilead! What bounty in a sin-sick, suffering world!

Just as sorrow comes to everyone, so does suffering. The saint and the sinner are consumed with it. We live with it. We die with it. Any pastor who has sat at a bedside, walked through a cemetery, or held a sobbing flock to his heart has heard the cry a thousand times, "Why, Lord? Oh, *why* this sorrow and this suffering?" The answer, compared to the soul-searching question, is relatively simple. *It is that we live in an imperfect world!* There is sin in the world; where there is sin, there are sorrow and suffering—often borne by the blameless.

This was *not* God's plan. He meant for the world to be perfect. He made it so. He meant for humans to be perfect. He made them so. If God's people could have remained perfect, in the Garden, there would have been no sickness, no sadness, no death on earth! But from the very first, people sinned against God. From that moment, the world was never perfect again. The imperfections that have developed are deadly. There are murders, mayhem, germs, and genocide. There are deformity and fear. There is depravity. There are poverty and pain. There are sick minds and sick bodies. Because Christians live in this imperfect world, they become part of the imperfection simply because *it* is here and *we* are here.

Christians develop deadly diseases, measles, and head colds because there are germs. They are killed in automobile accidents for the same reason they have flat tires: *imperfection* in either the machinery or human judgment. The fact that we are Christians does not lift our lives above the physical laws of the world.

Of course, God could prevent any or all of these tragedies from transpiring. He could reach down and take Christians out of each day's danger. And sometimes he does! Many times he does! We tend to forget that when we are asking, Why? We tend to forget the numerous times each day and night that we, and our loved ones, are saved from accident or death. How many times have you prayed, "Lord, my child is driving home from college today on icy roads! Please protect her"? Then the child arrived unharmed, perhaps passing on the way several accidents on those icy roads. How often have you held a loved one's hand, hot with fever, and prayed, "Lord, heal him"? And the loved one lived, while all around you in the hospital people worsened and died of disease. How often have you seen sadness and said, "Lord, lift it," and he did, or faced danger and cried, "God, help me," and he did?

But all of this protection, this healing, this help, is a "bonus blessing," above and beyond his promises. He never promised that Christians would lead healthy, wealthy lives. (If he had, and if it were so, the whole world would be Christian!) What he *promised* was peace in the midst of peril, courage for the conflict, strength for the storm, a song in the night! What he *promised* was to love us and to never leave us alone! What he *promised* was happiness, not health; wisdom, not wealth; learning to lean on him, not relief!

The Christian way of life is the best, most blessed way of life there is! It is abundant. Christians in the Western world are, more often than not, the healthiest, wealthiest, most successful men and women around! But Christians do suffer, and the suffering, the sickness, the sorrow *of itself* most often has no spiritual significance at all. It is simply the result of being imperfect people on an imperfect planet. What we *do* with the suffering—how we face it, what we learn from it, and where it leaves us—has spiritual significance!

Furthermore, just as Christians sometimes suffer by being in an imperfect world, so non-Christians sometimes reap rich benefits simply because the forces of good that God has set in motion touch everyone, the nonbeliever as well as the believer! God's miracles of the medical profession, for instance, will heal those who do not pray as quickly as they will heal those who do. The Bible says, "Your Father . . . sends rain on the just and the unjust" (Matt. 5:45). The fact IS that "Every good gift and every perfect gift is from above" (Jas. 1:17), whether it be the sunshine or rain, an advancement in medicine, a beautiful body, or a bright mind.

The *difference* in people is how they react to what has happened to them, whether it be success or sorrow. The non-Christian will use his gifts for himself. The gift will stop with him, stymied, and may not even result in happiness for him. The Christian, however, will know that his gifts are to the glory of God; he will use them as such, and the result will be his long lasting happiness, even to eternity!

To reap God's benefits is a rare and precious privilege, regardless of the nature of the gift. Once I sat all night long beside a loved one who lay in a hospital bed struggling to live. As the dawn of a new day streamed in the windows, I opened the Word and began to read. The Psalms seemed especially soothing, supplying me with words of prayer and supplication. Suddenly I stopped reading, staring at Psalm 68:19, "Blessed be the Lord, who daily loadeth us with benefits." I looked at the bed where the struggle for life continued. I was bound to that bed by my heartstrings. "Blessed be the Lord, who daily loadeth us with benefits." Lord? Is this my benefit for today? My *load* of benefit? Must the benefit be so heavy, Lord? Ah, but he knows, when, and to whom the load belongs! Thank him, in all things!

I used to think that we were thankful only for things that made us happy! Now I know differently, for I have seen sorrow be as big a blessing as happiness! I used to pass hospitals and say, "Thank God, we're not there tonight!" I used to pass cripples and say, "There but for the grace of God go I." But I have learned differently. Suffering can bring a beauty to life that would not have been there otherwise.

On our anniversary, November 21, several years ago, my husband and I were celebrating with a roses-and-romance dinner at the Old San Francisco Steak House. It was one week to the day *before* Thanksgiving Day. We happily counted our blessings as we looked forward to the holiday!

That same night in Lubbock, Texas, our son (then a student at Texas Tech University) became suddenly, seriously ill! Not realizing that he had more than "just a virus," William Jewell stayed in his room until Saturday night. But when his temperature shot to 103°, his roommate wrapped him in blankets, carried him to the car, and rushed him to the emergency room of Methodist Hospital. The roommate then called my husband and me.

By the time I reached Lubbock the next morning, our son had been moved into isolation and placed on the critical list. His skin was yellow. The tiny veins in his eyelids, wrists, and ankles broke open and bled without warning. His temperature continued to rise and his blood pressure to drop. On Monday morning the doctors called a conference. They were grave. "His liver is rapidly collapsing," they said. "We don't know why, and we can't reverse it. We suggest your husband come as soon as possible. We don't know what you are facing in the next twenty-four hours!"

I called Jewell in Dallas and found him already preparing for the flight to Lubbock. He was with me within a few hours. Throughout Tuesday and Tuesday night, we watched and waited as our son's condition slowly but surely worsened. Neither of us slept or ate. Finally, on Wednesday morning, the doctors were startled to see that our son's condition had stabilized—still critical but stable. It remained stable throughout Wednesday and Wednesday night, and on Thursday morning the answer to his condition changed dramatically! The mysterious malady attacking the liver had moved, of its own accord, from the liver to the lungs. The lungs were now impacted with viral pneumonia, but the liver was beginning to regenerate itself! There seemed to be no permanent damage done. Barring any critical complications, the convalescence would be long and languid, but he would live!

Shortly after we received this word, as we still stood in the hallway crying tears of happiness, the lunch trays arrived, each one laden with turkey, dressing, and cranberry sauce! *Dear God,* I thought, *"it's Thanksgiving Day! For the first time in my life, it's Thanksgiving Day!"*

Later I remembered that week in Lubbock, how we were brought together as never before, how we had felt God's presence and peace, how our son's faith had never faltered, and how we found beauty and blessing and love. I wrote these words:

> Oh, the blessing of the burden
>   That can cause a man to cry
> For the help of Someone stronger
>   On whose care he can rely.
> Oh, the beauty of the darkness
>   That can cause a heart to grope

For the light from heaven's windows
  And refreshing rays of hope.
For it's here, within the shadow,
  That we learn to look and live!
And it's here, within the sorrow,
  That we sacrifice and give.

So tomorrow, on the mountain,
  We can say of day's now dim,
"It was there, within the valley,
  That we learned to lean on him!"

I want, now, to write about a truth that I have only recently learned: we don't have to have a mountain to move before we go to God for help! He helps with *little* sorrows as well as with *big* ones!

Having lived through fifty years, one marriage, two children, several cities, and assorted friends and enemies, I have had few really big problems. But the emphasis is on the one word *few*. Looking back on half a century, I can count on my fingers the times I have faced life-or-death situations! That's enough, mind you. I'm not asking for more! But the fact remains that although I have experienced PROBLEMS, what I have usually had is *problems*, little letters! (Not that the little-letter problems don't give you wear and tear. They do. They work like the slow erosion of the sea on a sand castle. The constant washing of the waves wears the sand castle away. So it is with little, constant problems.) But regardless of the relentlessness of these *problems* in my life, they *were* the little-letter kind. For the longest time, I was reluctant to pray about them.

A rainy day might make me begin to feel really blue about one or the other of these constant *problems*. I would face the fact that there was no simple solution in sight, and it would make me so sad. I would wonder how to handle it all, what to say, when to say it. I would, without planning to do so, begin to tell God all about my blue mood, maybe even begin to cry a little. But then I would "remember my manners." All my Christian conditioning would come to the surface. There would be before me all those tried-and-true attitudes I had been taught from childhood. "Count your blessings!" "You can't be sad when you're being thankful!" "Look around you at the hospitals, the prisons, the unemployment lines. Now *that's* trouble!" Then I would feel a great guilt that my spirit had ever been frustrated or fearful or low. I would timidly take back my tiny burden from the throne of grace in order to give God more time to deal with death, plague, pestilence, or whatever was most pressing at the moment on his agenda. For years I allowed no little-letter problems to clutter up my supplications to the Almighty. I suppose I thought he would think me ungrateful for all that he'd given me. Or maybe I thought he expected me to be able to handle those things without him, what with my good mind and body and all. Or maybe . . . who knows? That's just the way I was. I did not hesitate to ask for his love, but I did not dare ask for his deliverance.

Dear Drew Ann, my daughter, put my feelings about little problems into perspective for me. She has a degree in psychology, so she is our family "sage." Actually, she was something of a sage before she went away to college. She has always been unusually perceptive of human situations. Even as a child she would startle us with her clear conceptions of people's feelings, their motivations, or their meaning. She could "read between the lines" better than anyone her age I've ever known. As she grew older, her interest in psychology was natural. Simply put, it is an interest in people and a warm awareness of their needs. Other children are natural tennis players, mathematicians, or musicians. Drew Ann *understands.*

One day Drew Ann and I were driving into downtown Dallas. (She was at the wheel. She does not trust me to talk and drive. Since it is folly to imagine my not talking from the house into town, she was driving.) On the freeway we fell into a serious discussion, something about one of my day-to-day dilemmas for which there seemed to be no solution. It was a relationship with a relative, a relationship with which I had lived for a long time. It was beginning to get to me. We discussed the cycle of events that kept recreating the dilemma. Soon we were into the center of the city, surrounded by cars and horns and signals. As we waited for a light to change from red to green, a mass of humanity crossed the street in front of us, people in all sizes and shapes, hurrying, scurrying about their business. Suddenly we saw in the middle of this humanity a girl about Drew Ann's age. She had lovely, light hair, and a clear complexion. She was beautifully dressed. She carried a small leather case and was obviously one of the young business women of which our city boasts. She was also crippled! One of her legs was twisted, turning in the wrong direction beneath her, making it shorter than the other. She limped, in a loping stride, one shoulder forced forward by the deformity, her face set purposefully on the light, being sure she made it across four lanes in time.

Instantly upon seeing her, my heart melted. She was so beautiful. She was so successful. She had overcome and now competed in a world full of people who could walk without thinking. She was also somebody's daughter! My eyes grew misty and I said, "Oh, dear, how brave and beautiful she is, and how it must break her mother's heart! Now *there* is trouble! I don't *have* any troubles."

Drew Ann patted my hand and replied, "That's right,

Mom. She has a *big* problem, and you have a *little* problem, but don't dare discount it! It can be significant!"

I was startled. *Significant,* what an interesting word. Why had I never thought of it? It was like a light turning on somewhere! Significant! I had assumed I was *in*significant. I had been timid with my tiny sorrow. I was wrong!

Drew Ann continued to talk. "I've often observed this in people," she said. "They think they could, or should, handle some problem themselves because it is so small a thing. But from what I've been taught, and from what I've seen, I know that little things can become big things overnight and, therefore, cannot be taken lightly."

She was right. Whether in psychology or theology, little things cannot be taken lightly. Indeed, *God* does not take them lightly. "I know when the sparrow falls," he said (see Matt. 10:29). Let me tell you about sparrows and the spirit of God. All of God's creations, and especially God's creatures, reflect his face and the heavenly hand that made them. Those who study the habits of these creatures tell us that the more intelligent animals are legend in their "love" for their masters. The horse, the dog, that "loves" will fight viciously to avenge that master and will die to protect him from hurt and harm. This "human" trait in animals has often been romanticized by writers and movie makers. But there is another, more intimate trait in animals that is not as often noted by laypeople. It is that many animals mourn their mates, as surely and as sadly as do people. Even in the wild, we are told, elephants will actually shriek in grief for a lost loved one. Gorillas, too, live in family groups and show grief.

Birds grieve too. I had never seen this phenomenon until recently. I knew, of course, that birds mate and build nests together. I knew, too, that they feed their young and teach them to fly. When I was a little girl, my grandfather had told me that birds mourn. He had told me of the farm and the surrounding forest where he grew up and of the blue jays that lived in the orchard. It was the blue jays that held the loudest funerals he said, gathering together in a tree over the dead bird's body and screeching for hours with sounds and cries and calls unlike any they make at other times. But I had never seen it and assumed I would not since I was a "city girl." (To tell the truth, I wondered if Grandfather's imagination might have confused fact with fancy!)

But I am here to say that I have seen it now, and in the city at that! One day in June, I drove down a street lined with trees and grass and gardens limp with the summer sun. The houses were locked against the glare. No neighbors were out and about. I hurried through the heat to buy some fruit, something fresh to put before the family at dinner. I could see the heat rising in waves from the pavement, and suddenly I saw a sparrow. He was standing in the middle of the street, a little to the left of my car. As I drove past him, he did not move. The wheels must have been within a few inches of him, but he did not fly away, indeed, did not even flinch. There was something small and still lying beside him. Was it another bird? I couldn't believe it. So startled was I that I stopped the car at the corner and turned around.

This time I drove slowly back to the bird and stopped beside him. My heart broke. A dead bird lay near, her neck broken, but otherwise still beautiful. Her mate stood beside her. The pavement must have been hot. His breast heaved rapidly as he breathed. Other cars besides mine had undoubtedly come as close to him. But still he stood, waiting for her to raise her head and fly away with him. I wanted to pick him up, to take him with me. But I left him there with her, mourning. Strangely enough, I have seen the same thing twice since then: once in another neighborhood, and once on the boundaries of a busy freeway where the sound and the wind of passing traffic must have been suffocating at ground level. But nothing drove the mourners to leave the loved one until the mourning was done.

"I know when the sparrow falls," said God. The sparrow reflects the spirit of the Maker who cares about even his smallest creatures (Matt. 10:29). Do not be timid about your tiny sorrow. Take it to God. He has time. He may take your sorrow away entirely, or he may give you more endurance, but he will deal with it. Nothing is ever too small for him! It is significant!

14
Heaven-sent Assignments

Crosses are very real. They are a fact of Christian life that I have finally learned to accept. I used to think that crosses were figurative: the "burden" of being a Christian in a sinful world; the "hardship" of the ups and downs of marriage; the "stress and strain" of raising children; having to "put up with" cantankerous people or employers or mean church members. I have learned differently. Each Christian is *called,* or *assigned,* a cross or crosses to bear. God does not give crosses, as such. He gives assignments!

Sometimes these assignments are happy directives that give us pleasure, peace, and accomplishment. We are prepared from birth to fulfill these assignments—the businesses we are to begin, the mates we are to win, the children we are to raise, the books we are to write, the clubs we are to lead, the sales we are to make! From the beginning we have the ability to attain the top in whatever great and glorious assignments he has for us!

But sometimes his assignments are difficult, even to the death; and if we carry out the assignments willingly and well, they become crosses upon which we are crucified. God did not say to his only Son, "Go to earth and be crucified!" He did not give his Son a cross. He gave his Son an assignment. "Go to earth and save men from their sins," he said. So Jesus came to earth. He was born as a baby, and he lived and laughed and loved among men as one of them. He taught them, persuaded them, and displayed his power for them. But with words and wonders he could not win the world. With miracles he could not win the world. With parables he could not win the world. For the world went on its way, not listening to his love. He had to sacrifice himself! There was no other way to carry out his assignment! He had to die. In the dying, he had to take upon himself the sins of all this world. He could see that we could not save ourselves from ourselves or our sin. *He* had to accept the sin—the pain of it, the sickness and sorrow of it, the death of it—so that *we* could accept *him*. He was our only salvation. Jesus Christ, Son of God, carried a cross and was crucified upon it. *But the cross was not the end in itself! It was merely the means by which he completed his assignment from his Father!* Thus it is with the Christian child of God! Our assignments also can become crosses!

Incidentally, a Christian cross is something quite far and away and different from divine punishment. In fact I feel that very rarely does God point his finger at his children in punishment, He *does* punish, of course, at certain times, under certain circumstances. He took David's child. He refused to let Moses enter the Promised Land. He turned Lot's wife into a pillar of salt. He allowed the Israelites to be enslaved and then let them wander in the wilderness for forty years. But I believe God's punishment is rare, just as his wrath is rare. "For he is slow to anger," the Book reads. (And thank heaven! We would all be in *plenty* of trouble with an impatient God!)

What we see sometimes as "punishment" is actually the consequence of sin. For instance, if we commit adultery, we are going to have broken hearts, broken homes, and children who are emotionally mixed up. If we lie, the "truth will find us out"; we will be embarrassed. If we bear false witness, we are going to lose friends, family, and our credit rating. If we are continually covetous, angry, greedy, or grudging, we are going to get ulcers (or at the very least, acid indigestion). If we murder or smoke too much or drive when we're drunk, we are likely not to live too long. But God has not punished us! We have perpetrated the tragedy upon ourselves.

I remember a play presented by the young people of our church. One by one they came down the aisle, bringing with them their crosses. The crosses were all different shapes and sizes. There was a delicate little gold cross with a tiny diamond in the center; there was a heavy, rough-hewn cross, almost life-size; there were crosses of marble, alabaster, sandalwood, and lilies of the valley. Each Christian brought his cross to the altar and told of the burden he bore, how long he had carried the cross, how hard and heavy it was. The Christians were tired and so they had come together at the altar to exchange their crosses. They laid down their crosses and picked up others, examining them, turning them, twisting them to the light, listening to the hardship of the one who had shared the way of that cross. At last, each Christian picked up his own cross again and carried it away, convinced now that God knew best his ability to bear a cross, how heavy or how light it must be and how lasting. Not one had been given a cross he could not bear.

When God makes assignments, they are beautifully balanced with equal portions of burden and ability. I believe firmly that the Lord, in his loving foreknowledge of life, prepares each one of us especially for the burdens that we will be called upon to bear! Just as we are given special talent and intelligence to reach the glorious goals he has led us to attempt, so we are given special traits and attitudes that are designed as tools with which to work with whatever is to come. We are prepared, by birth and experience. If our burdens are to be physical, we are given extra strength. If they are to be emotional, we are given extra stability. If ours is to be a sudden situation, we are given the inborn ability to cope in crisis. If ours is to be a long-lasting burden, we are prepared, by birth and by experience, with stamina and "stickability"!

If the crosses we bear are God's assignments, we are assured of the special preparation, the special traits and attitudes, that will enable us to carry them well and to be witnesses. But I believe that many Christians are bearing burdens, being crucified on crosses, which God never meant for them to have. They were prepared by birth and experience for something else, but somewhere along the way they stepped out of the *center* of his will for their lives. You see, whatever the choice, however large or small the decision, if it is not God's *perfect* will, we cannot possibly be *perfectly* prepared for the problems we will encounter in the course of that action! This does not mean that God stops loving us or that he will leave us. He will be with us and continue to use us, even in *secondary* places of service; but those will not be his best, most beautiful plans for us. Our burdens will be much more awkward than the ones we would have borne in his *first* place of service!

In a certain congregation, there was a lovely young woman. She was willowy with dainty, delicate features. Her face was framed with a cloud of dark hair, and her eyes were those of a trusting, beautiful child. You wanted to love her, to protect her, to take away any tears. She was married to a brilliant scientist, a young man who had been sought after by several research and development centers. She had four daughters, all school age, all beautiful and brilliant. But her husband, who was good and kind and considerate, was not a Christian. It was not that he had not heard the Word. He had, many times in many ways. But as a scientist he felt he could accept nothing on faith. Science and religion were poles apart he reasoned, and he rejected religion. He refused to come with his wife and their children to church. He did not forbid her or the children, but he was unhappy to be left alone on Sunday. He said so, to her, to her parents, and to any of her Christian friends who would listen.

One day this young man became a sad statistic, one of the millions of people in America who suffer from cancer. For several years we watched the sorrow of that family, as the young father lay dying, unable to protect and provide for his loved ones. Finally, just a few weeks before he died, he accepted Jesus Christ as his Savior. We rejoiced with the young mother and her children. We wept with her at the funeral, we cared for the children, we collected money for household accounts. But in the months following, we watched helplessly as she collapsed, mentally, emotionally, and physically. She was ill for a long while. During that time she lost her home. One daughter was almost mortally injured in a motorcycle joyride. Another daughter married in haste and unhappiness. The other two daughters struggled through their youthful years, borrowing money, working nights and studying days, never knowing the security of a father's support or the freedom to date, party, or play. Some of her friends cried and questioned, "Why has God dealt so with this precious, praying child of his?"

I had met this young woman's parents. They told me something that made me wonder if all their daughter's suffering was part of God's assignment for her. Years before, they told me, when their daughter had introduced them to the young scientist, they had seen she was serious about him then. Therefore, they began to pray with her and with him. They presented to him the plan of salvation, and he refused to take the step of faith. They brought the pastor to the young man. The pastor was persuasive, pleaded, and prayed, but still the young man refused to take the step of faith. Then the parents began to counsel with their daughter. "He is not a Christian," they said, "and he actively rejects Jesus. You have always wanted a Christian father for your children, a Christian home, a church related life. You cannot have all that with this young man in the foreseeable future. Please pray further, before he leads you to the altar."

"But I love him so," the daughter said.

Her pastor also counseled. "Be ye not unequally yoked together" (2 Cor. 6:14), he reminded her.

"But perhaps I am the one to lead him to the Lord," she said. "Perhaps I am his chance for a changed life! He will be better with me than with anyone else!" she said.

The pastor replied, "There is no doubt that the Lord longs for him to be a believer, but there are literally a thousand ways for the Lord to woo and win this young man. That is the Lord's business, not yours. Your business is to obey the Lord's divine directive. The Lord's directive is plain. It is that Christians must not be yoked with non-Christians in marriage."

"But I love him so," the young woman said. And she married him. She lived with him, and she loved him until the day he died, and God continued to use her. She won her four daughters to Christ, and at last the man she so loved came to Christ also. God never left her alone. *But she was not prepared* for the burden of her husband's lengthy illness and death. She had not been born with the physical or mental stability to stand. She collapsed.

I came to ponder the possibility that these were burdens she was never in this world meant to bear. Had she been married to God's *first* choice of a mate for her, she would have faced problems and pain, certainly, for these are facts of life. But they would have been ones she could carry, assignments she could fulfill, for they were meant to be hers!

Being absolutely in the center of God's will assures us of the proper preparation for our problems! *Wherever* we are, there will be mountaintops and valleys, trouble and trial, and failure and success. That is life! But *within* God's will, we have the tools to reach the mountaintop and the "rod and staff" to carry us through the valley. *Without* God's will, we may find ourselves at a loss, literally, for some of our resources. It is vital, then, that we visualize every daily direction we take in the light of the Lord's leadership, for then we can accept his assignments with assurance!

(If we come to this conclusion in our young years, wonderful! If we are middle aged before we begin this way of life, still wonderful! No need to worry about "wasted" years from a "wrong" decision somewhere way back when. The Lord knew precisely the day, the hour in your life when you were going to begin living for him completely, and he has plans! Turn it all over to the Lord, *now,* the past, the present, the future, and let him lead you from *now on*!)

There are times when we do not see assignments as heartbreak or burden when first we accept them. We accept them gladly, gloriously. But as we continue to carry them to final fulfillment, we see that they are going to require of us our all. We see suddenly that we must lay our all on the altar of sacrifice and service just as Jesus did.

I remember a childless couple with such a sweet, sweet spirit. They wanted so much to have the pleasure of parenting. Finally, after disappointing diagnoses from an array of doctors, they turned toward adoption. How they prayed that God would give them the perfect child for them, at the right time and place, that their personalities as parents would match completely the needs of the child that was to come to their hearts and their home. In time the Lord led them to this perfect child. They felt so assured, so confident that in every way this was his will. How happily they took their son home and settled him in his room, and how they loved him all his life. He was handsome, talented, and intelligent.

The year that he was to graduate from college, he felt faint. They feared for his health and took him to a team of doctors. They learned that their son, the light of their lives, had leukemia. For many months he fought for his life. The parents were wealthy and were able to spare no expense. They never considered that they had made a mistake so many years ago. They thanked God that they, who were strong and healthy and wealthy, had been chosen to care for that boy through life and death. They dedicated themselves to him for months, desiring so to do it. But as they watched him, sick and suffering, the assignment, which they had accepted as a glorious gift from God, became a cross on which they were crucified. Although it broke their hearts, they carried the cross willingly and well.

The three of them were the most marvelous witnesses to the glory of God the community had ever seen. Countless people were blessed to see them stand so straight and strong in the face of such sorrow! Many were brought to Christ by their example! Through that cross, there was a crown! That father and mother came away from their son's funeral with glory on their faces. They had been so near to God for so many months! How often have we heard the words, "Nearer, my God, to thee, . . ./E'en tho it be a cross That raiseth me"! The cross and then the crown. It is a fact of the Christian life!

Now and then, however, we refuse to face this fact, and we forfeit the crowns. We are humanly afraid. We see the assignments for what they will be, for what they will become—crosses, and we refuse to accept them. We are creatures of free will, after all, and we can choose to walk away from God's callings. Ah, but then we are left bereft, for without those crosses we are never the men and women we were meant to be, never completed, made spiritually perfect as God intends us all to be! How much we miss, what time and opportunity we lose, being *less* than the Lord means for us to be!

Let me tell you a story about bearing burdens that came out of Radio Free Europe during the days of WW II. The war was well advanced, and Austria was under the direct domination of the Nazi army. Only the underground had any contact with the Allies, and its members were in desperate danger. Still they operated, almost underneath the feet of the Nazi army, faithfully leading groups of refugees in twos, threes, and tens across the mountaintops into Switzerland!

One night a group of refugees began to gather at the appointed place. They materialized separately from the shadows: a husband and wife, lovers, two brothers, an old man, a mother and her small child. Each carried a bundle of belongings, all that he would take with him into freedom. The stronger ones would be asked to carry also parcels of provisions, for the climb across the mountain would take two days. The guide, a hardened leader of the underground, leaned against the pile of provisions as he watched the refugees gather and huddle together in the darkness. It was as if he were evaluating each one for strength and stamina. He began to assign the burdens each one would carry. Finally, only the mother and child and old man were left. He placed a parcel of provisions on the mother's shoulders and then he lifted the little girl from her arms! "The old man will carry the child," he said.

The group began to protest, "But he is old! The child is too heavy! We should lighten his load, not add to it!"

But the guide was stern, "The old man will carry the child," he repeated, as he strapped the little girl to the old man's back.

They began to climb, through the night and into the morning. It was obvious that the old man was exhausted when they stopped for breakfast beside a tumbling stream. "Let one of us carry the child or the mother's parcel of provisions so that *she* can carry the child," they pleaded.

The guide was firm. "The old man will carry the child. You each have your own burdens, but the child is *his* responsibility."

The climb continued. The old man stumbled and fell, faltering again and again, while the child slept peacefully on his back. The guide was always near and saw to it that the path was clear; but he never relented, and the old man was not relieved of his burden. Two days, forty-eight hours, of climbing, slipping, sliding, and finally, when they were all ready to faint with fatigue, the guide pulled each of them through a tiny pass between the rocks! They were at the peak! Below them lay Switzerland!

"Look," said the guide. "Freedom!"

They rested there at the top of the mountain, looking down at their freedom. The child awoke and climbed down from the old man's back. She played with his hair and beard and kissed his weathered face. He wept a bit and whispered, "I would never have made it without you, my beautiful little burden! I would have died along the way. I expected to. I never expected to make it all the way across the mountains. But he made me carry you so that your life depended on mine! I had to stay alive, at least this long, and now I see, it is *you* who have saved *me!*"

The guide smiled. His decision had been sure. His intuition had told him that the old man would not make it across the mountains, certainly not without some incentive greater than himself. Clearly, his burden had become his blessing: the old man was alive, and freedom was before him!

And so it is, and has always been, when God gives his children burdens to bear. He knows what we can carry and why and when and how far! And he knows that only in bearing the burdens will we reach the magnificent mountaintops he has for us! It's all a matter of definition, really. *We* call them "burdens." *God* calls them "blessings"!

We would not want to leave this assessment of God's assignments without affirming once more the JOY of the vast *majority* of divine directives. God means for us to have life and to have it abundantly and to come rejoicing! He gives us a voice and tells us to sing! He gives us a canvas and tells us to paint! He provides a young pastor with a church and tells him to preach, a young doctor with a patient and tells him to heal! Most of God's assignments are meant to make us healthy, wealthy, wise, and wonderful! Accept those as readily as you do the directives that will create crosses in your life!

Did you know that there are people who simply cannot accept success, happiness, health, and wealth? Psychologists have found this to be one of the most pronounced human phenomenons! We live in a land that was founded on the laboring class, and until this present generation we were all taught that gain must not be ill gotten! "Nobody gets something for nothing," we were told. And (although this *present* generation sometimes seems to feel a bit differently) by and large, even in this day and time, people *want* to work and are *willing* to work for the symbols of success as they see them. They work, and they work well. They reach the top of the mountain. *Quo Vadis?*

Only when people feel that the fruits of labor are deserved can they accept them thoroughly. Often, however, we feel unworthy of these "fruits." Overnight-success people are particularly prone to associate guilt with gain. Most people are simply unprepared for success. They feel frightened. "This is too good to be true," they wail; and like Henny-Penny, they walk around wondering when the sky will fall.

God never intended this terror over a simple thing like success. Of course, sometimes we don't deserve it! One of the things I have learned in the last fifty years is that life is not fair. Sometimes you get trouble you don't deserve, and sometimes you get success you don't deserve. But God allows what he will. And if today you have success, accept it in his name just as you did salvation, which you also did not deserve!

The Christian has the most simple solution here, for the Word tells us that all good gifts come from above and are to be used for God's glory! What joy, then, to return a portion of time, talent, and monetary resources to him, the source of everything! Be joyful! What fun to use your influence for him! Be glad! You do not need to worry that other people are having to use their sorrow for him, while you are having to use your success. At this moment success is your assignment. Maybe tomorrow sorrow will be your assignment, maybe not. That is not your worry either. Your only obligation to God is to do the best you can, with what you have, where you are today, and today you have success. Be happy!

Having been brought up in the home of a minister of music, I never knew what wealth was. (Being a minister of music in Mississippi fifty years ago was a labor of love, and if you got money for it too you were way ahead of the game!) I knew the Scripture about how hard it is for a rich man to get into heaven's gate, and it made me glad I didn't have much money.

Then I grew up. Money didn't seem such a hardship after all. Now I live in Dallas where money is a common commodity. There are more millionaires here than you can count and many, many more people who simply have lots and lots of money. A mighty number of these people are consecrated Christians! Praise be!

Lots of money still startles me. When we first moved to this city and to this First Baptist Church, I was startled all the time. Mercy! Suddenly I saw what marvelous things money can do for the cause of Christ! I know people who's monthly tithe is more than my father made in a year. I know a woman who personally sent a planeload of supplies to the Rio Grande Valley for flood victims. I know a man who furnished a whole hospital floor in honor of his wife for her birthday. I know couples who spend several weeks each summer at their own expense working with our missionaries in the Far East or Europe or South America. The plane fare alone, for the two of them, would provide a sumptuous time in some vacation paradise, but they give it to God and always claim they've *gotten* more than they've *given!* It's marvelous what money can do!

These same people have beautiful homes and big cars and cattle ranches and condominiums in Colorado; and they use it all for the glory of God! They are magnificent witnesses to the world. Christianity is successful. It is exciting. It is happy. With their lives, they are saying, "What I have is his because *I* am his. If tomorrow all of my world as I know it were washed away, *I* would still be his, and I would be happy!" It is not that these people do not have worries. They do. I know a number of them personally, and they bleed when they are wounded and weep when their hearts are broken, even as the rest of us do. But they also *accept* success, health, wealth, or whatever because that is what God has given or allowed in their lives. They do not need to feel guilty about their gain, for it is God's glory!

As for me, personally, wealth was never one of my problems! I've never had oil or cattle or land. But I do have happiness, and would you believe that for the longest time this was hard for me to accept? In my younger years, when all was well, I used to wonder if God would ever find me trustworthy enough to be tried. Now there is no more need to wonder. My half century has not been without heartbreak. I faced it boldly! Heartbreak was an assignment I accepted! But with happiness I was very shy. How long would it last? Was it mine to keep, or must I give it back? There was still so much that was unsettled in my life. How could I be happy today when I didn't know about tomorrow? And most importantly, why did *I* have all these things—a loving husband, beautiful children, independent parents, work to do that I adored—when people who were dearer and sweeter and better had lost one or all of these things? Why should *I* be happy?! I walked all around happiness, and I reached out and touched it timidly. Should I embrace it? There was so much sunshine, but surely somewhere it was raining, and surely somehow I should be worrying about that!

How foolish I felt when finally I realized that this timidity to touch was not a God-given attitude. It was an encroachment on my Christian life by Satan himself! You are saved and successful, and the sun is shining. If Satan can take away your peace and your pleasure and your happiness in it, he has diminished your life considerably. Don't let him do it! "Ye are the light of the world" (Matt. 5:14), remember? Don't let him dim it! He can't take away your rewards in heaven. Don't let him take away your riches on earth!

God held out salvation to you, and you accepted it. He held out sorrow to you, and you accepted it. Now he holds out happiness to you! Trust it! Believe it! Embrace it! With the same bold abandon that you accepted the blessings of heartbreak, you accept the blessings of happiness. I have learned to do it! Whether it be for many months or for a day or for a few minutes, when happiness touches me, I take it!

These are God's heaven-sent assignments!

15
Emotional Trial and Error

I was in my early twenties when I realized that I could be a candidate for the psychiatrist's couch. It's not that I'm *disturbed,* you understand, just emotionally STORMY! (The symptoms can be the same, believe me!) My moods can go from monsoon to placid in less time than it takes to issue a weather bulletin. My highs are mountaintops, and my lows are deep, deep valleys. I feel everything so . . . seriously! Whether it is my happiness in my husband or my satisfaction with my work or my awe at the granddaughter in my arms, I feel it *seriously.* Salty, French-fried onion rings are devastatingly tasty to me. Bluebonnets and black cows scattered over a hillside in summer are breathtakingly beautiful. A child's sadness is unbearable to me. Angry words cut me to the core, and I feel physical and mental pain. Sometimes it seems that I live my life in capital letters! It sounds exciting, and it is! But there are so many times when I wish that I could make a decision logically, without my love getting in the way, or calmly plan the pattern of my days or arrange the rhythm of my years. But I am not ever going to be "cool"! It is simply not my nature! (Now my husband, by nature, is so deliberate as he manages his life that even his *mistakes* are methodical!) But

I ride the roller coaster of emotion, and I have had to learn to hold on to my hat! After fifty years, it is still STORMY— thunder and lightning and tiny tears in the night over nothing and everything.

But I am here to tell you that in the middle of all this emotion which will always be a part of me, I have *perfect peace*, in mind, heart, and soul. Praise him! If I have a Christian testimony it is this: *God has saved me not only for eternity but also for now!* He claims me, calms me, and he holds me in his hand not only for then but also for now; the wonder of it overwhelms me! Without him, my life in eternity would be lost and my life here on earth would be a senseless shamble!

I wish that I could explain to you the trauma of living with a "nervous nature." You've heard of hair with split ends? Well I have nerves with split ends, frayed, frazzled, and flapping in the wind! I was born with them. When you are born with high voltage in your veins, your body chemistry is constantly boiling, like the proverbial "caldron of spirits." You always run, not walk. You do things in a hurry whether or not there is a *need* to hurry. You naturally hurry. You want everything *now*: the finished piece of needlepoint, the painted front porch. If you could, you'd read the first and last chapters of a book simultaneously. And before long you've blown a fuse! My husband is an electrical engineer, and he tends to talk in those terms. "What is the matter with you," he will wonder. "Are your circuits overloaded?"

That is as close to describing it as you can come. One minute you're ON, with all your connections wired. And the next minute you're OFF, no current anywhere. It can be funny, it can be sad, it can be debilitating, and *that* is where the danger lies. When there's a weakness, whether it be in body or mind, then *that* is where you are going to need God to survive.

Why? Because Satan knows your weaknesses and strengths very well. Once your soul is safe with God, Satan will do everything possible to ruin your effectiveness as a person, a mate, a parent, and certainly as a Christian. Have you read Ephesians 6:12 lately? If you have, you know now where the *war* is and with whom! Satan will ruin your witness as "surely as sin" if he can, and he will do it with your own weaknesses!

In areas where you are naturally strong, Satan doesn't bother you, of course! Satan never tries to tempt me with alcohol or tobacco. I hate the taste and smell of both, and cigarette smoke gives me a headache. It would be a waste of Satan's time to tempt me with cocktails. And Satan does not bother to tempt me with pecan pies and cream cakes. An abundance of sugar makes me—What was grandmother's word?—*bilious!* (I think that means you are yellowish, a little dizzy, and want to lie down.) Anyway, desserts are no "devils food" for me. And adultery is just too much trouble. I can't manage the man I've got. Two would be one too many men. No temptation there.

But, Satan can tempt me into a tizzy with no trouble at all. The result is far from funny. Satan knows my nervous nature, and he uses it time after time after terrible time to make me less efficient, less effective, and eventually (if I would let it continue each time) much less healthy than I can be if I am calm.

Often when I awake in the morning, my first thought will be the multitude of things that I must do that day. I will have knots in the back of my neck before breakfast. The fact that I adore everything that I'm doing makes no difference. The fact that I'm happy about everything that is happening to me does not matter. I still have knots in my neck. This is uncomfortable to say the *least*. (You simply cannot be at your best with knots in your neck!) At the *most* it can affect not only your body but also your mind. Your mental attitude becomes one of fear and frustration. As you fight it, you realize that the haste is from within, not from without, and then the anxiety settles in.

I learned a long time ago that this was Satan's greatest tool with me. This was the weakness that would ruin my witness if I let it. People who are paralyzed with anxiety, fear, and frustration are very surely removed from service to themselves and to the Lord. Anxiety, fear, and frustration are born of a nervous nature like mine. Therefore, I could see clearly that this was what Satan had in mind for me. I could also see clearly that this was not *God's* plan for me. Suddenly, I realized that I was in the middle of a power play between Satan and the Lord! Satan and the Lord were doing battle, for *my* mind and emotions! As soon as I saw this, I saw also the outcome. If Satan and the Lord are doing battle, we all know who is stronger! The outcome is bound to be a victory for the Lord! What a relief! The fight was no longer mine alone. It was the Lord's, first and foremost, and at once I saw myself winning instead of losing. If God be for me, who can be against me? Satan might as well turn tail and run!

Sometimes I have a mental picture of the Lord Jesus standing between me and that fallen angel Lucifer. It's a beautiful sight, believe me. What I want most in the world at that moment is peace, of body and mind, and see, I am being protected by the Prince of peace himself! As I go about my day I can delight in it, free from fear and frustration and, most specifically, knots in my neck! The fact that calm natured people do not have ulcers, migraines, and mental anxiety is no matter. The fact that *I* do not have ulcers, migraines, and mental anxiety is an absolute *miracle* of God's grace, and I give him the glory!

There are people, of course, who need the care and counseling of a physician and/or psychologist. But there are many more, like me, who are simply pawns in Satan's war games against God and the good that is in us. If he can disable or disarm us in any way, God cannot use us. If he can prey upon our weaknesses, whatever they are, long and hard enough, he can rob us of our witness and ruin our lives.

Sometimes the temptation is so subtle we don't realize it as such. I remember reading in one of our inspirational magazines about a young man who had been blessed with a beautiful voice. He was asked to sing at many church and civic services. But the young man was terribly shy. Soon he developed a devastating case of stage fright. For days before a performance he would be unable to sleep or eat. There came the time when he began refusing any and all requests to sing. But, even this did not free him, for he simply exchanged one debilitating symptom for another. He became consumed with guilt. He was a Christian. He knew his voice was a gift from God, and he had always wanted to find and follow the Lord's will. Instead, he had stopped using his talent entirely.

After weeks of soul-searching, he came clearly to the conclusion that his stage fright was not a normally shy reaction to a public performance. Rather it was the weakness that Satan was using to ruin his witness! Suddenly he saw himself on God's side of a war. With the power of the Almighty, literally, he won! Gradually the stage fright left him and was replaced with a wonderful joy in the preparation and in the performance of his music. His was a ministry that touched many lives for the Lord!

There are many weaknesses that Satan can use, things we might see as normal reactions to certain circumstances unless we recognize the continuing battle to remove us from service. Perhaps being shy is not your problem. Perhaps feeling inferior is your problem. Perhaps the desire for personal possessions is your problem. But whatever it is, recognize it as Satan's tool in your life, turn the battle over to the Lord, and prepare for eventual victory! It's like walking on the water. As long as you keep your eyes lifted to the Lord you need not fear or faint or feel inferior!

I *love* this line from an unknown poet: "Sometimes I calm the storm! But sometimes I let the storm rage, and calm my child!" You, too, can walk on water!

Remember, also, that faith must be reaffirmed. Just when you think you will never again fall prey to your problem, your frailty, suddenly you do. With me, for instance, that perfect peace of body and mind can continue for months at a time, and then one day the knots are in the back of my neck again! That's when I turn to all the precious promises in God's Word, all those passages that I have lined and lined and relined through the years. Do you know how many times the word *peace* is used in the New Testament? I tried to count once and gave up! Countless, countless times God wrote that word for me! "For God hath not given us the spirit of fear; but of power, and of love, and of a sound mind" (2 Tim. 1:7). "Thou wilt keep him in perfect peace, whose mind is stayed on Thee" (Isa. 26:3). "The peace of God, which passes all understanding, will keep your hearts and minds in Christ Jesus" (Phil. 4:7, RSV). "The peace that Christ gives is to guide you in the decisions you make" (Col. 3:15, TEV). On and on he reassures the soul: I made you! You are mine! I will not let you go! I want you to witness for me; therefore, I will protect you from the powers of darkness and despair!

That's not for eternity, that's for now, and when I look up

from these words the sun is shining! A lovely little chorus goes, "I could only offer Him my brokenness and strife, . . . But He made something beautiful, of my life!"

Lord, I love thee!

16
God's Garden

There is a precious place on the grounds of Ridgecrest Baptist Conference Center in North Carolina. It is called Johnson Springs, and it was there that I learned to pray.

The story of how Johnson Springs came to be is very beautiful and very sad in the way that good-byes can be sad and beautiful at the same time if the memories are sweet! The spring of crystal clear water, almost hidden by the oleander bushes, was found many, many years ago by a little boy named William Johnson. His father was a Carolina pastor, and the two used to walk in the mountains around Ridgecrest long before it became the nation's largest Christian conference center. Upon their discovery of the springs, father and son decided to clear the underbrush, to clip the rhododendron bushes, and to make a miniature waterfall with rocks, thus directing the water so that one could easily fill a cup and drink. "I want it to be a place where people can come when they're thirsty and rest," said the little boy. And so father and son did all they could that first summer, planning to return the following summer to complete the project. Eight months later, however, just as they were looking forward to their return to the retreat, the little boy's life was lost in a sudden fire that swept through the big, wooden school building where he studied.

The father's grief was very great. In his heaviness of heart, he knew that he must make something good from his sorrow in memory of his son. He returned alone to the mountains and to the spot where the springs came clear and cool and fresh from the ground. He cleaned the ground around the springs, made the miniature waterfall, and built wooden benches and a brush arbor. Then he dedicated it all in the love of the Lord. It was called Johnson Springs, Garden of Prayer.

This place of prayer has had a special meaning to the many college students who served in the summers as Ridgecrest staffers. The guests, thousands each week, were at Ridgecrest for only a few days. They visited the springs perhaps once or twice during their time on the mountaintop. But we staffers, college kids who cooked and cleaned and led hikes, were there for three months. Johnson Springs became our holy ground! Here the prayer services were held. Here we introduced Christ to friends who did not know him. For some it was a place of happiness and thoughtful thanksgiving. For others it was a Gethsemane, as they decided for or against God's will in their lives. And, as I've said, for me it was the place where I learned to pray.

I had been a Christian since childhood. I did not doubt my salvation. But life was simple, and so far there had been no tears or trauma. Praying was something my parents did. Suddenly, in Johnson Springs, it was something *I* did. *Praying became personal to me,* and I began to know the deep, abiding, abounding joy that I have known ever since in the Lord. I settled my life in Johnson Springs! The decisions that I made there are with me today, thirty years later. I learned not only to pray but also to listen to the Lord, to harvest from his word his message to me, to open my heart to his leadership. I learned that often his answers are sudden, and that just as often there is an answer you are not meant to know at that moment.

One night I went to Johnson Springs quite late. It was August, and the summer was almost over. There was a certain decision that I thought I had to make before I left Ridgecrest that summer, and I planned to stay in the garden that night until I had my answer. I read, prayed, and pleaded with God. Finally, on my knees, I told him I would not let him go until he led me to a decision. Still there was nothing in my heart to fill my need. I raised my head. My New Testament lay on the bench beside me, and I opened it once more at random. The lanterns strung through the trees gave light, and I read, "I have much more to tell you, but now it would be too much for you to bear" (John 16:12, TEV). My heart stood still. *Dear God! That you would speak directly to me with your Word!* It was unbearably beautiful! The fact that he had not led me to a decision that night no longer mattered! Nothing mattered, except the exciting experience of having a direct conversation with God, the Creator! From that moment on prayer has been the most positive force in my life.

Prayer is probably the most personal experience a Christian has. Therefore there are as many ways to pray as there are people. My parents, for instance, approached prayer differently. My mother was a natural student and teacher, and she spent long hours in Bible study. Her prayers were very practiced, and she verbalized them during those long hours with the Word. She thought through her prayers and often talked aloud with the Lord. My father, however, was rarely still long enough to study. His days never ended at 5:00 PM. There was always a music committee meeting, a service for which he must lead a song, a choir festival. Yet he carried his prayers with him continually. He used to say to me, "The earnest desires of my heart are my prayers, for my music and the people of Mississippi. My whole life is a supplication." He prayed for me in the same way. He wanted the world for me. When he thought of me every thought was a prayer, the earnest desire of his heart.

A philosopher once said, "The greatest prayer is patience," and perhaps that is true: the patience to "let go and let God."

To some people *poetry* is prayer. To some people *service* is prayer. I love the lines written by a harried housewife, "Although I must have Martha's hands I have a Mary mind, and as I shine the boots and shoes, Thy sandals, Lord, I find! I think of how they trod the earth, what time I scrub the floor. Accept this meditation, Lord, I haven't time for more!"

To some people *song* is prayer. Since those summers at Ridgecrest I have had a beautiful friend named Barbara whose brilliant voice has graced the greatest music halls of the world. From the day of her debut at Carnegie Hall, she has been in demand and has blessed Christian crusades far and wide with her music. She is married to a Scot, who was one of the foremost organists in Scotland before they moved to America. One day she heard him playing the small organ in their home, playing and singing to himself one after another of the old, old hymns of his homeland with his heavy Scottish brogue. She slipped into the room to listen, silent and unseen. After a time he finished with a simple melody, and as his hands fell still he bowed his head, "This is my praise, Lord! My prayer to thee!"

And there are times when *silence* is prayer. (I think sometimes that it is only the noisy person who can properly appreciate silence. Silence is an absolute elixir to me!) Often, as we approach prayer, we are silent because we do not know what words to say. The pain or the problem or the suffering is so overwhelming we cannot comprehend it, much less conquer it. God knew that there would be times so terrible that we could not find the path to prayer. Thus he sent the Holy Spirit to commune with him for us. What assurance when we read in Romans 8:26: "The Spirit also comes to help us, weak as we are. For we do not know how we ought to pray; the Spirit himself pleads with God for us in groans that words cannot express" (TEV). Silence! Sweet, sweet silence is prayer also!

Printed in a book of devotions for each day is a poem by an unknown author:

> Far out on the sea there are billows
>   That never shall break on the beach
> Just so are the songs of my silence
>   That never shall soar into speech.
>
> The thoughts of my soul that are harbored
>   In solitude, quiet, and unheard
> Are dreams, and a quest, and a vision
>   Too lofty for language or word.
>
> Do you ask why the peace of this silence?!
>   Why the heart feels release from its care?!
> Because here there is more of God's presence
>   And here there is answer to prayer!

Ah! The final word with any prayer, ANSWER! There is *always* an answer! That is because the Person to whom we pray lives, and he listens, and he loves us enough to *always* answer. Sometimes it is now, sometimes later, sometimes yes, and sometimes no! But he always answers within his will, which is good because God is good!

Have you noticed how many times *you* are the answer to your own prayers? God has no better agent to bring about his answer! Robert Schuler, famed pastor of the Hour of Power, tells of growing up on a farm in Iowa. He and his father and his brothers would leave the fields at noon to gather around the table together for the midday meal. His father prayed both before and after the meal, before to ask God's blessing on the food and after to thank God for his goodness. By the time the second prayer was offered, the father was already thinking of the work that waited for them in the fields, and the horses that would soon be hitched up again. And so his "after" prayer was sometimes short and sweet, "Thank you Lord for thy abundant blessings! Boys, hitch up!" Pray, ask for God's guidance and then get going! *You* can often be the answer!

As for me, personally, prayer is intense and totally private. I have friends who practice conversational prayer in groups of from two to ten people. It is a beautiful blessing to them. I have other friends who find great comfort and faith in prayer and share groups. But this is not the way for me. Certainly I pray fervent, heartfelt prayers in public. Surely I shall pray with a friend who is in sorrow, or beside a sickbed, prayers of hope and courage and conviction. But when I "meet the Master face-to-face," I must be alone.

There has to be that time when I can be totally honest, without hurting someone; totally "weary of well doing," without tarnishing my testimony; totally fearful, without frightening those who love me; totally guilty, seeking forgiveness before God. I must be able to weep if I want, to cry out to him, and then to just listen for as long as it takes! "I come to the garden alone," the song says, "And he walks with me, and he talks with me, And he tells me I am his own." Perhaps it is that I must have him all to myself at that moment, for oh, how I need to know that I am his own. This, to me, is prayer. Personal! It is like the twenty-third Psalm, "The Lord is *my* shepherd; . . . he leadeth *me* . . . He restoreth *my* soul: . . . Surely goodness and mercy shall follow *me* . . . and *I* will dwell in the house of the Lord" (author's italics). Personal, very personal!

The Lord Jesus himself depended on prayer, and it was one of the most important glimpses of glory that he gave to his disciples, this communion with God, the Creator. He took them up on the mountainside, and he said, "After this manner therefore pray ye: Our Father which art in heaven, . . . Give us this day . . . . deliver us from evil: For thine is the kingdom, and the power, and the glory, for ever" (Matt. 6:9-13). A perfect prayer!

Through the years we have called this the Lord's Prayer. We have been wrong. Jesus gave this prayer to his disciples. It was a prayer to be prayed by believers, followers, devotees of the faith. It was not *his* prayer; it was theirs.

But there *was* a prayer that was prayed by the Son of God himself, by our Lord, when no one else listened; for he was alone. It was not to teach or to train that he prayed that night, nor as an example of the "more excellent way." It was as a brokenhearted Son, bent, bereaved, fearful, pleading to be released from a burden so heavy he felt he could not bear it. He went to Gethsemane, and all night long he laid before God his fear and his dread, "O my Father, if it be possible, let this cup pass from me," for he felt he could not bear it. But as he lay still upon the ground, with the blood and tears mingled on his face, he spoke the final words, "nevertheless, not as I will, but as thou wilt" (Matt. 26:39). And that, Christian, is "the *Lord's* prayer"!

There was, in a certain church, a choice child of God, a man whose music was truly "soul music," for it was inspired with the love of the Lord. This man was taken from service suddenly because of an irreversible virus of the brain that left him unable to be the person he had been. Stunned, his choir went to their knees. His church contacted other churches, which contacted other churches, which contacted other churches, and soon the entire Convention was praying for this man. Chains of prayer around the clock continued in many cities for many months. If ever the gates of heaven were stormed, if ever the throne of grace were besieged, it was for this beloved man. And believers would weep at testimony time and tell how they had "prayed all night, claimed the promises, and therefore had faith" that this man would be restored to stand once more in his appointed place.

But! This is not the final word of faith. This is not all! Pray we can, oh, yes! Claim the promises, have faith in God's unfathomable grace, oh, yes! But in the end, we must pray the *Lord's* prayer, "Nevertheless not my will, but thine, be done" (Luke 22:42).

God's will was done with that choice child of his; he was not restored to stand among us. We have accepted this will because we see we must.

The Lord's prayer, you must know by now, goes farther in faith than the disciple's prayer! The Lord's prayer says: *Without* my daily bread, thy will be done! *Without* deliverance from evil, trial, or trouble, thy will be done! *Without* my health, my husband, my money, or my lifelong mission, thy will be done! This is the prayer we must pray if we pray the Lord's prayer!

Oh, God, it is not easy. Oh, it is not simple. Oh, sometimes, it is so impossible. Our only hope is to hold to the knowledge that *he* knows what is best for us, that *his* way is best for us, whatever, wherever, whenever! And if we hold hard to this knowledge as the storms toss and tear us apart, perhaps we will learn to pray with Jesus, "Father, . . . nevertheless not my will, but thine, be done" (Luke 22:42).

Prayer, a most precious lesson in life!

The joyful song of learning never ends. (You never know when you've learned *enough!*) So you keep on learning, realizing all along how little, indeed, you do know! At least when you're *old* you realize that! But when you're young . . .

My first summer in North Carolina as a Ridgecrest staffer was my twentieth summer! I was a college junior, soon to be a senior! How sophisticated I was, thirty years ago! Because there were three hundred staffers, college students from all over America, the special speakers for the week would often meet with us on Friday night for our camp fire service. It was a time when they could shed the formality of the pulpit and share with us our fun, as well as our serious moments. On one such occasion Dr. Chester Swor, Christian writer and lecturer and nationally known counselor of the youth of the land, was with us. At the opening of the camp fire service, I, as an officer on the Staff Council, was to give a brief statement of my Christian beliefs and then introduce Dr. Swor to the gathering! I was proud to be in such a position! This was illustrious company! Also, I had listened and learned from this man all of my life, literally. He, as a young man, had lived in the same, small Mississippi college town as my mother. Later he had taught in that town and in that college. He was something of a legend in Mississippi, and I looked forward to meeting him at the camp fire!

And so at testimony time, I spoke for about five minutes. Dr. Swor spoke for about forty-five minutes. And all too soon it was time to go. As we were leaving the camp fire, I approached Dr. Swor companionably (such liberties I took then) and began to walk along with him. He was walking carefully, with the cane that has become such a part of his colorful character, and he was being courteous. He patiently asked about my parents, and then he complimented me on the things I had said at the service.

I was so excited! "Oh, Dr. Swor! I'm so glad to hear such encouragement from you! You know, I've got a stack of stuff under my bed, programs I've planned and devotionals I've done; someday *soon,* I'm going to sit down and *write a book* about *life!*"

I have since been grateful he did not laugh out loud. (Well his eyes *were* twinkling, but then they always twinkled.) "Now Miss Joy Durham," he said, using my middle name that is the same as my mother's, "that is a book I really want to *see!* But promise me one thing! Promise me you will wait until you have learned a little *of* life before you write a book *about* life!"

"Oh," I nodded wisely. "Well! How long do you think I should wait? Until I'm twenty-five?"

He answered, as solemn as a sage, "My dear child! When you have lived for half a century, then, *perhaps,* you will be ready to begin to *contemplate* your book!"

Well, I am one half a century old, and what do I know now? More than yesterday, less than tomorrow, and that I like to learn! I know that I am proud of every year that passes! Proud of the experience, the pain, the pleasure, the *progress!* For I've found out:

Youth is fascinating, Maturity is fulfilled!
Youth is becoming, Maturity is beautiful!
Youth is brave without thinking,
Maturity is brave because it *has* thought!
Youth can press toward the mark,
Maturity can attain!

God knew best! There is a season for all things! A time to be born, a time to die; a time to weep, a time to laugh; a time for sunshine, a time for rain; a time to sow, a time to reap! This is my time for reaping. Thank you, God.

My father had a saying he used when he had made a mistake—"Live and learn!"

End of Love Letter

There is nothing new under the sun. The Bible tells us so in Proverbs. Nothing new—because it has all been said. Succeeding generations simply express it differently, with a sense of discovery. Even with the Good Book, there are several ways to put things.

In front of me on my desk is a row of Bible translations. There are the old American Standard Version and the traditional King James Version. I rarely read the King James anymore. Those were the words I read as a child, and I know them so well. Sometimes *The Living Bible* seems more "alive." My favorite is *The Amplified Bible*. But really the Bible hasn't changed that much. Somebody has merely said it differently—with a sense of discovery.

So . . . I know. There is nothing new in *A Woman's Song*. It has all been said somewhere, sometime before. But I, Joy, have made all these discoveries myself—through the years and the tears and the continuous flow of my life. "Cry me a river," the song went . . . and I have! "Smile, and the world smiles with you," they used to sing . . . and I have!

So can you!

If I have worded it differently, so it seems like a sudden discovery to you, I'm joyful. If I can tell you what I've seen of suffering or joy or sorrow or husbands or of being a wife or a woman full of pride and pleasure—so that you may see it clearly—I'm so glad! If I can make one day easier for you, (because I've been there too), if I can shed one ray of insight for you because I've shared, if I can reinforce your faith or enhance your hope . . . I'm so thrilled.

You have a friend. I love you. And I am always

"Joy" fully Yours —